SMALL BUSINESS FOR THE REST OF US

SMALL BUSINESS FOR THE REST OF US

ONE DUDE'S JOURNEY

BY BENNIE POLLARD

for Mom

TABLE OF CONTENTS

ACCORDING TO THE SMALL BUSINESS ADMINISTRATION, A SMALL BUSINESS CAN EMPLOY UP TO 500 PEOPLE.

This book is not written for people in companies of that size. In my industry, the beauty industry, the majority of hair salons employ between six and eight stylists. This book is for the entrepreneur-driven small companies of two to fifty employees. These businesses are the backbone of our country.

They are the Mom and Pop shops that were started by someone with a passion, someone who had a dream and little to no money.

I have observed these businesses rarely sustain a successful record. The trouble is that passion doesn't equal mastery. Many small businesses come and go so fast; snap your fingers and yesterday's salon has become a bakery, then a florist, and then a tattoo shop.

To create something, and keep it going, requires intention and leadership. Individual circumstances don't matter; however, individuals do. It was vision and persistence that made me a success. I did not inherit a fortune, nor was I bestowed with exceptional luck. My origin story was challenging; my young adulthood was meandering and full of missteps. Despite that, my business earned its first million in revenue when I was thirty. God willing and the creek don't rise, everything will continue to grow.

Much of my business knowledge comes from personal experience. I have intentionally included a good deal of my biography in order to demonstrate how my methods evolved and because you may recognize yourself in that youthful scrappiness. Though I'm a voracious business book reader, the strongest, most important lessons I have learned came from my own mistakes. My hope with this book is to impart to you a sense of your own value. I want to inspire you to reach for your dreams, and to give you the knowledge I gained from my mistakes.

This book will differ substantially from your average business book. I'm not going to throw meaningless jargon at you in the hope you'll think I'm impressive. I'm going to tell you my story—my whole story, so you can see yourself in it too. Along the way, you will find the nuts and bolts: everyday practices that those experiences prompted. And because I believe in inspiring people, you will also find motivational boxes.

I have earned significant success in the beauty industry. I say that not to show off, but to show you that if someone like me could succeed, you can too. The lessons and ideas I'm about to share with you transfer far beyond the world of salons and haircuts. In fact, I retired my chair at the salon to have more time to speak to business owners like you. As I'm delivering seminars, it's common to look up and find a veterinarian, a dentist—even a Harley Davidson dealer—in the audience. An attorney friend of mine once said, "I never thought I would learn so much about business from a hairdresser."

It doesn't matter the size of your goal; it could be to break $200,000 or your first million or beyond. If you're trying to improve your small business, read on. This book is for you.

SMALL BUSINESS FOR THE REST OF US

CHAPTER 1

TRAUMA AS TEACHER

I WAS TEN YEARS OLD WHEN MY MOM SHOT MY DAD AND KILLED HIM. NO ONE WAS SURPRISED.

The night it happened, I was in the house. So were my two brothers and two sisters, but none of us woke to the shot. I heard nothing until my aunt shook me gently and whispered, "Bennie. Can you go up the back stairs and sleep up there?" The rails were off the stairs for a project of some kind, so she warned me to be careful as I walked outside to get to my grandmother's upstairs apartment. Upon opening the back door, I remember seeing flashing blue lights. "What the heck?" I wondered. There were police cruisers in the yard, and officers were crawling all over the place. But I was tired and groggy. At age ten, all I wanted was to go back to sleep.

It wasn't until the next morning that I heard a partial explanation. My uncle had driven in from Tennessee during the night. He sat down with the oldest kids: my brother and sister and me. He said, "Kids. Your daddy's dead." This led to more questions for which there were no answers. He told us our mom wasn't around just then. There was crime tape across the living room door. And my mom wasn't home. I was scared.

A few hours later, Mom came back. I went over and sat down with her. Then I turned to her, "You did it, didn't you?"

"Yeah," she said. He'd hit her for the last time.

* * *

5

Like most people, my parents were my first teachers. I had one inspiring role model in my mother. And one horrific, what-not-to-do example in my father. One of my earliest memories of my father revolved around him threatening us from the back porch—the family bird cage in his hand. A little green parakeet trembled inside.

A belligerent alcoholic, my dad was usually fried out of his mind. Though my parents were divorced and lived separately, they somehow kept trying to get back together. The apartment where I lived with my mom and siblings was in the lower portion of a duplex. My grandma, Mimi, lived upstairs, and we kids often went back and forth. The night of the parakeet episode, Dad had pushed my mother beyond the limits of her patience. He had been beating on her in the preceding days. I could still see the big red marks on her neck from where he'd hit her. She'd told him to go, but he still somehow managed to have a key to the downstairs apartment. So, Mom, the four other kids, and I were hiding upstairs, because we figured he'd probably come back again.

Sure enough, Dad banged into the house. We heard him stomping around, looking for us. The next thing we heard was him banging on Mimi's door. "Let me in! Nancy, I want to see my kids!" We looked through the window of the door and yelled for him to go away. We saw our dad standing there, looking deranged in the yellow pool of light from the porch bulb. It was a cold night. His breath fogged as he stood on the porch, dangling the metal cage from his hand. "This parakeet's gonna die if you don't let me in." I think he knew right then that we all valued that bird's presence over his.

I felt baffled by his behavior. I even asked my mom, "How am I supposed to feel about that?"

"I don't know," she said.

Mom was eventually exonerated in my dad's death. She claimed self-defense, and no one disputed it. Nor should they have. There were multiple, documented cases of beating after beating. It seemed like her trial and probation were a mere formality, and everyone was relieved that someone finally took the asshole out. Looking back on those events now, I remember everything felt very surreal. It took a long time before the new reality of my life would set in.

Forty-five years have passed since the night Dad died. It was confusing in our house, as a kid. I was the oldest of five and carried my father's name, Bennie Pollard. I am junior to his senior. Not every memory of my dad was terrible. There were blips of happiness, like the time my dad and I were out driving, and he stopped to get cheeseburgers and Lay's Potato Chips with me. But most of the time, I remember him as cruel and scary.

MOTIVATION
TRIAL BY FIRE

Some people might say my alcoholic father doesn't belong in a business book. I disagree and here's why.

My childhood was challenging—to say the least—but honestly, I look back at it now as one of the most important things that ever happened to me.

Why? First, I'm alive. If my father's life hadn't ended when it did, who knows how bad things would have gotten. I am grateful for my life and for my mother, who likely saved me from further harm.

Second, going through that gave me such courage and strength. Sometimes, early trauma handicaps people. They end up fearful and avoidant. I was ten when my dad died. At the time, I was just trying to survive. In the pursuant years, I *was* angry, but—ultimately—I emerged from my youth tough as nails. I think about those events this way: If I can go through that and survive, then bring it, World. I can survive anything.

1. You can also survive anything.
2. Hard times make you stronger.
3. Sometimes trauma is the best learning tool you have.

CHAPTER 2

ADVENTURES OF A SNOT-NOSED KID

TO EXPLAIN WHAT MY LIFE GREW INTO AFTER MY DAD'S DEATH, I NEED TO TELL YOU MORE ABOUT MY ADVENTURES AS A SNOT-NOSED KID.

Looking back, it seems as though I was a born entrepreneur.

At age seven, I lived with my mom and dad in Louisville's south end, in an area called Valley Station. It was a blue-collar, working-class area, but I didn't know that at the time. Everybody there was working class, so all of us had hand-me-down clothes and busted toys. I walked several blocks to school every day, starting in the first grade. There was no lunch money at our house. There were baloney sandwiches or whatever Mom could pull together in a bag for lunch. No one had spending money either, but once in a while Mom would put a few M&M's in a bag for dessert.

Every Wednesday, my school showed a movie after school, usually a Disney film. One day in second grade, I desperately wanted to go see that week's movie, but we didn't have any money for it. It was only thirty-five cents; it might as well have been a million dollars. I remember sitting there in the lunch room, surrounded by classmates and feeling frustrated about the movie. Then, I don't know how, I just started selling my M&M's, two for a nickel. Pretty soon, bam! I had enough for a movie ticket.

I felt surprised by the discovery. "Wow, that worked!" I didn't know it at the time, but I had taken the first step toward entrepreneurship. Selling those M&M's was my first taste of commerce.

The movie, "My Side of the Mountain", is about a boy who grows weary of his dad making false promises to take him camping. He runs away, goes out in the wilderness, and learns how to live off the land. He creates a whole home for himself in a hollowed-out tree. It was so empowering to the second-grade me, a kid who burned to do more, to be more. My M&M's sales and getting to see that particular movie slid together into one word—independence. Even though I got in trouble for getting home so late, I thought it was the coolest thing in the world.

* * *

After Mom and Dad split up, we were living downstairs in a duplex; Mimi lived upstairs. Sometimes an aunt and her kids lived there too, including Scott, who was a cousin about my age. We used to run around in the neighborhood together, gathering glass bottles for the three-cent return deposit at the grocery store. I remember the weight of those 7-Up and Pepsi bottles in the eight-pack carrier. Each filled slot meant we had almost enough to get a ten-cent soda for ourselves. On a good day, we could each have our own, with a few cents left over for candy.

While hanging around the Kroger grocery store, we realized that bottle collecting was small potatoes. The real opportunity was staring us in the face. In those days, the store wouldn't let their shopping carts leave the store, because they kept getting pinched. So, folks would get a couple of heavy bags of food and have to carry them out to their car by themselves. Or, we figured, we could help them out...for tips, of course. We made bank. Remember: a sixteen-ounce soda cost ten cents. So, if someone handed us a whole dollar?

"Oh my God!" we'd say. Though Kroger's eventually ran us off —"Kids, you're not supposed to be here. You're not old enough,"—even with that indignity, hustling felt good to me. It provided a means to supplement my boloney-sandwich diet. More than that, I realized I could earn money by myself.

These childhood memories occurred in Kentucky in the early 70s. Where I lived in Old Louisville, there were the fancy mansions—and then there were the neighborhoods of falling-down,-shotgun houses where the labor force lived. The neighborhood in which we lived continued to get increasingly more rough, by the day it seemed. My mom finally decided to move her babies out of the broken-down duplex and away from the troubled neighborhood, the same neighborhood she grew up in. Somehow on her limited education, working full time, and raising five kids, she figured out how to get a low-interest loan directed toward single mothers.

On a quarter-acre lot, thirty minutes outside of Louisville, Mom had a brand-new house built. It was a brick, three-bedroom, one-bath house built from scratch. And she put her babies in there. I look back at that now and think, *Good God! How did she do that?* These days, when I hear people crying about how hard life is, my mom springs to mind. Someone is telling me a sob story about how they don't have enough money or time, and it's just not fair, and getting ahead is impossible...in my head I'm thinking, *Quit your crying.*

MOTIVATION
NO FEAR IS MORE THAN A SLOGAN

Hard things are attainable. In fact, the word impossible is not in my vocabulary. What I'm about to say to you next might sound stale.

So what?

Your attitude about your problems is the determining factor in whether you will get past them. As Henry Ford said, "Whether you believe you can do a thing or not, you are right."

Maybe you're trying to climb higher in your industry, or maybe you want to switch career tracks entirely and build your dream job. I'm here to tell you that based on my experience, my mom's experience, and so many others' that I have been a part of: **It doesn't really matter where you come from. Think through whatever your goal is, swallow the fear, and freakin' go after it!**

A lot of times, would-be entrepreneurs nurture a dream. They sit on it until the right moment—but they don't ever launch. Why? Fear of losing money. Fear of criticism. Fear it will be imperfect. I'm here to tell you that all those things will happen. They happened to me too. I have lost money; I have boatloads of critics; every business I ever launched had flaws in it. You can't wait for the vision to be perfect. It won't ever be perfect. You just have to commit to being in that space and course correct as you go.

1. Kick fear in the ass.
2. Mistakes will happen; you cannot avoid them. Learn from them.
3. Commit: you can have fear—or fear can have you.

I was eleven when we moved out to our new house on the exquisitely named Flatlick Road in Bullitt County, Kentucky. Sounds like a country song, doesn't it?

The change solved the problems that bothered my mother: there was less crime, and the newly constructed house wasn't constantly falling apart like the old duplex. And there was a lot of wide open space in which to play, which should have been a bonus for me. Except ...

There were no aunts and grandma to act as backup babysitters (except one summer when Mimi lived with us). That left...me. As the oldest child of the family, I got left in charge of the other four kids. All day, every day, in the summers, I was babysitter-in-chief. My buddies were walking down the street, guitars on their shoulder, forming rock bands—and trying to figure out how to be men. I wanted to do that too, so badly. But I could not leave the yard. So, I used my best sales skills to get them to come and hang out with us.

"Come over here, guys."

That worked sometimes, but not always. I felt like I lost two summers at the critical ages of twelve and thirteen, and I resented it. My younger brothers and sisters knew that. They didn't like it any better than I did.

Regardless of the difficulty, my mom did provide some opportunities for me out on Flatlick Road that I couldn't get in the city, and I'm grateful for that. I got to play Little League Football. I still don't know how Mom got the money for the equipment; I think maybe some of the neighbors pitched in together and got me a helmet and pads. It turned out, I was really good at football. I played

Little League, in junior high school, and then about a year in high school. I started at tackle and kicked everybody's ass. I loved it.

One of those kindly neighbors was Woody Parish. He had some farm land that he worked at a bit. He had a hell of a garden that wasn't big enough to qualify as a farm, but it was close. He spent his days working a little and nights sitting around on the porch, drinking beer with his brother and friends. I can still remember the ruckus they made out there just drinking beer, hootin' and hollering'. Nothing crazy, mind you—just old guys drinking beer.

He was one of the most giving dudes I ever saw. The whole neighborhood, they recognized they had this single parent over there with all these babies. I'm pretty sure that group of people were the ones that made football happen for me. Then one summer morning, first thing, here came Woody with his tractor and his disk. He went back and carved a big old chunk in the back of the yard. I'd never seen any equipment like that before. The disk would turn these great big pieces of dirt—wide as a table—and he'd pull it and flip it upside down. It was the coolest thing. And then he'd come back with his till to break it up, and he'd make his rows. He did all this for free, just to help out this new neighbor, Nancy Carol—get her garden going so she and her kids could eat.

I thought that was all pretty exciting until the next day, when Woody showed up with a load of horse manure and said, "Get over here, boy." Woody was putting me to work. I had to break up the horse poop by hand, which was both gross and cool at the same time, but it sure made the garden grow.

Mom wanted the usual vegetables planted. So, Woody showed me how to grow potatoes, tomatoes, corn, cucumbers, and beans. Then, for the rest of the summer, it was up to me and my brother to keep it watered and weeded. We hated all that work. Back in Louisville, there was no cutting the grass or weeding the garden. My brother actually broke a couple lawn mowers, just so he wouldn't have to cut the grass. There was one reward for all that hard work that has served me well: a warm tomato picked right off the vine and eaten like an apple. It's off the charts.

My brothers, sisters, and I would eat off the garden all summer. There was very little meat at our house (except baloney, but I don't count that as meat). Instead, we made summer sandwiches, which were sliced cucumbers and tomatoes on toast. I still like to eat those now.

Mom's sisters eventually realized the genius of her escape from the city and followed suit, moving onto Flatlick Road as well. Aunt Doris and my mom would get together at summer's end and can like crazy, preserving the harvest into winter. We'd have all these mason jars full of green beans, potatoes, and pickles—all kinds of stuff. So, we always had plenty of food. There was never any cash around, but we always had plenty to eat.

* * *

About the time Woody was finished with me, another neighbor came by to talk to Mom. He wanted to help supplement the income of this fatherless family. "Nancy, let me take this boy over here, and we'll give him a little work." His name was Lonnie Grisby. He was there to initiate me into the crew of boys picking feed corn in his field.

Out into the cornfield I went. The rows and rows of corn plants were just turning a light brown color. They were drying out nicely. Green corn leaves can be a little sharp. Dried corn leaves are *really* sharp. I was out there with some cheap cotton gloves on and short sleeves, because I would die in long sleeves. (Kentucky in August is humid as hell and about ninety-five degrees, which feels like 110-plus.) So, for a dollar an hour, I'd pick the corn and get covered in little bitty paper cuts. Then I'd start sweating, and they'd sting! It was hard work.

But it paid off when I got my first paycheck—twelve whole dollars—I could finally participate in the bell-bottom jeans trend. If you wanted to be somebody in 1976, you had to have bell-bottom jeans. And then, miracle of miracles, Mom had a good week at the salon and bought me my first pair of Converse Chuck Taylors: green low-top sneakers. They were seventeen dollars at the time, which was a freakin' fortune, because the dollar store tennis shoes were only one dollar. Together with my bell bottoms, I looked good. I felt like I could hold my head up high when I went skating at the roller rink with friends. The skaters went around and round to "The Joker" by Steve Miller Band or "Dancing Queen" by Abba, and I could participate, because I finally had some money in my pocket. Money meant freedom to me—and I didn't ever want to be without it again.

I learned in those years that if I wanted more than what my mom could afford, I would have to work for it. I began to realize that if she gave me five dollars, it would be for milk and bread for the house and nothing more. I think Mom wanted to give me more money for fun; she just didn't have it.

So, when the opportunity to help bring in the hay harvest was offered, I said yes. The other younger kids and I weren't allowed to run the baler. Instead, we were the ones walking along, picking up the bales, and putting them on the truck. Then, we'd go over to the barn and throw bales into stacks. That was physical work—I mean, we were working our asses off in the heat for $1.50 an hour. At that age, I had grown to over six feet tall, but still didn't have a hell of a lot of muscle on me. Throwing hay definitely helped me build some.

Next, I got recruited to work tobacco—more tough, physical labor. We would first walk through the fields of six-foot tall stalks and sucker the tobacco plants, which meant we had to pinch a secondary stem off that was trying to grow. By removing those buds, I guess the plant would direct its growing energy to the existing leaves. We would get all sticky from suckering.

When the plants were big enough for harvest, we would get our tools: a big old tomahawk-looking tobacco knife and a sharpened stick that would hold the plants separate from each other for drying. First, we would jab the stick into the ground. Then, we'd put a little cone spike on its tip. Then, you'd lean over and tomahawk the tobacco plant—*thwack!* and, using both hands, spear its stem on the stick. Every stick would hold about six or eight plants. Some of the time, I got to harvest myself, but—being just a part-time helper—there were other guys who could do it a lot faster. So, if all of them were there, my job was to pick up all finished sticks, take them to the barn, and hang them.

A tobacco barn's apex, in the Ohio Valley, in the dog days of summer, might be the hottest place I have ever been. Four tiers tall, all that late summer heat rises and concentrates at the top. So, of course, that's where the tobacco needs to go first. Which means hired labor like me needed to climb up and hang it from the rafters. It was hotter than hell up there.

After the tobacco had cured, our crew was needed again to come strip the plants. It was near winter by then, so we sat near the covered wood stove with our hands making three piles: trash, lugs, and tips. Lugs was all the money, the trash got less money, and the tips got even less money. This process may have changed some in the years since I had the job, but one thing remains constant. Even now, though I have long since quit smoking, I love the smell of a barn full of drying tobacco that's just about cured. Sometimes, riding my motorcycle through the countryside, I can still smell the scent. I can't tell where the barn is, but the scent of nearly-ready tobacco makes me smile back on the boy I once was.

NUTS & BOLTS
WORK HARD

I attribute my work ethic to my mother and those kind neighbors. Growing up, I watched Mom go off to work at a salon. All day she stood and cut hair. When she came back home at night, she would still have to cook and clean and take care of her babies. She never stopped moving. So, when opportunities to work came my way I thought that was normal—that's just what you do. You get out there and work hard.

These days, I find a lot of so-called motivational business books and speakers preaching about working smarter. When I hear people say, "Work smarter, not harder," I say bullshit. If you work harder, you will always beat your competitor. Always.

Does that make us hard workers workaholics? No. It does not. A workaholic continually slaves away, mostly for appearance's sake. A sixty-hour work week means nothing if it's random and scattered. Running around putting out fires all day will get you exactly nowhere. A hard worker has a plan, a strategy for improving. A hard worker stays in the game while at work. And then, if you're a hard worker, you can walk away at the end of the day feeling accomplished and deserving of that ride on your Harley Davidson.

1. There's nothing wrong with sweating to make a living.
2. Beware of business gurus trying to sell you slogans and snake oil.
3. Work hard...with a plan.

All that sweating and laboring was good for me. I'm appreciative of those neighborhood dudes who cared enough to show me how to put in a day's labor. In those teen years, I also had the opportunity to tag along on some union jobs.

For about three years, my mom was remarried to a man who worked as an industrial paint contractor. He and the crew would go into these factories during the maintenance shutdowns and they'd have to paint everything, top to bottom. At age fourteen or fifteen, I'd already proven I wasn't afraid of a day's labor, so I was hired on as a helper, because of my stepdad's connection. Because this was union work, the men were probably making about sixteen to eighteen dollars an hour. They paid me five dollars an hour, which was incredible money to me. A couple of summers in a row, I got paychecks as big as $250 or $300 each. In the late 70s, that was serious money—buy-my-own-car kind of money.

I was glad for the income, but I also learned a whole lot about the kind of work I never wanted to do. Being in those factories was beyond nasty. One of them was a meat-packing factory. The smell was stupefying! And the dangerous chemicals they were spraying back then—epoxy paints and such—would fry anyone's brains.

Part of me realized this type of work would put me in the same position as my dad, Bennie Sr. My dad had been an auto body mechanic. Before he died, he was using some of the most lethal solvents and paints known to man, with only a paper mask for protection. This was prior to strict OSHA and workplace safety standards. Before he'd even cracked the first beer of the day, he was already fried out of his skull. I realized then that his work with dangerous chemicals contributed to his unfortunate life. And I wanted no part in a career like that.

CHAPTER 3

FIRST JOBS CAN FORM YOU

AT AGE SIXTEEN, I LEFT THE NEIGHBORHOOD LABOR POOL TO WORK MY FIRST "REAL JOB".

Instead of getting farm money for odd jobs, I would now be washing dishes for a paycheck at the Wildwood Country Club in Louisville. I can say with confidence that Wildwood changed my life for the better. I met a lifelong friend there, Danny, and my first professional mentor, Mr. Griff.

Mr. Griff was an elegant man who ran the restaurant at the country club. He wore a suit every day and kept the dining room humming along seamlessly. I think he served as the Wildwood maître d' for something like thirty-five years. He was the king of kings and set the tone for the whole staff. Confidence. Pride. Friendliness. It didn't matter who you were, Mr. Griff projected those attributes, always. I remember walking up to him in a shy manner saying, "Hey, Mr. Griff, can I have a smoke?"

He said, "Well, why do you have to be all shy about it? Just say, 'Hey Griff, give me a cigarette.'" This was Kentucky in about 1980. Everyone smoked, even in the restaurant kitchen.

I took pride in my job as dishwasher. It was my job to wipe down the whole kitchen at the end of a shift and mop the floors, which I did to perfection for three dollars an hour. Was it always fun mucking greasy floors and scraping food off pots? No. But that's just the way I am. I'm not capable of showing up and half-assing anything.

Any restaurant that serves French fries in the dining room will have grease on the floor in the kitchen. It's just how deep fryers work. So, I paid extra attention to that the fry-station floor, so no one would fall. As a precaution, it was laid with a wooden grate instead of tile to keep the slips to a minimum. It was an extra challenge to mop that, but my floors were clean enough to eat on by the end of every night.

And yet, I still took the blame when one of the cooks insisted on wearing his platform, disco-pimp shoes to cook in. I wondered what the hell he was wearing. (I had often looked askance at the choice.) Yes, it was the end of the disco era, but those were dancing shoes, not standing-on-a-wooden-grate shoes. So, when the guy's platform heel got caught in the grate, he fell and burned his hand on the griddle. Not long after, the restaurant manager, Miss Lu, came roaring into the kitchen and tore me a new one for not keeping the floor clean enough. I knew the fall wasn't my fault, but I didn't say so. Instead I said, "Okay, fine. I'll make sure."

That was my first experience of getting clocked for something that wasn't my fault. It wouldn't have been very strategic of me to argue back. I already knew it wasn't my error, and I also knew Miss Lu was responsible for the cook's behavior and performance. She was yelling at me, because she didn't want to own the mistake of mismanaging her employee. As an adult looking back now, I think about that incident this way. Sometimes shit rolls downhill, and that time it was my turn to suffer. It happens, and if you spend all your energy defending yourself, you can't move forward. Moving forward was my main goal at Wildwood. I didn't really care what Miss Lu thought of me; Mr. Griff was the person I was trying to impress. I admired him so much.

Before my job at the country club, I didn't know much etiquette. We were taught at home to say please and thank you—and that was about it. I'm glad I got those lessons, for sure. But it had never occurred to me there could be more to it. If our family went out for dinner, we went to White Castle or Burger Queen. All these rituals and specialized silverware at the country club were mysterious to me. It was like I had discovered a royal castle just down the road—with a completely different way of living.

One day, I happened to be passing through the dining room before the dinner hour. Mr. Griff had the serving staff gathered around a table. They were all in their uniforms. He was teaching which fork to use for what, which spoon to use for what, where the different glasses went, and how you moved toward the table. Oh, it was beautiful. It was absolutely, stunningly beautiful. I never even knew that kind of etiquette existed. At home, if a person wanted a fork, they opened the drawer, and fished around until they found a fork. Whatever fork they got a hold of was the one they used.

Upon seeing the demonstration, I was like, "Wow, what in the hell is all that crap for?" And then I thought, "I want to be a part of that." I knew there was something special happening in the dining room. I also realized there could be more money out there, and maybe there was something to learn from being exposed to the country club set.

After that glimpse of the table setting lesson, I went up to my new idol and said, "Mr. Griff, if you ever have room in the dining room, I want to grow up to do the bussing thing." I kept showing up on time and doing the best work possible as a dishwasher. Then one day, I was loading clean glasses onto the top shelf of the dish station. Mr. Griff walked up to the other side of the counter, leaned down to look at me under the glasses, and said, "Hey, you want to go out in the dining room?" I can still see the wide lapels on his 1970s suit. "Yes!" I said, with a big ole' grin on my face.

NUTS & BOLTS
ASK

Sometimes employees slave away, doing anything and everything asked, expecting that the next step up the ladder will be handed out as a prize for all that effort. I have also seen several people passed over for promotion who could not figure out why. I'm here to tell you that there are no fairy godmothers flying around in the work world. If you have a goal, you need to tell your boss about it.

Ask for what you want. Then, continue excellence at your current rung.

Once you're no longer a teenaged dishwasher, the challenges and responsibilities get trickier. Maybe you don't even want to stick with your company, but the same general rule applies. Figure out what you want, and then let it be known. Share that dream with trustworthy people who will support you and can help you network—and perhaps even finance you. The point is, you have to use your words and **state the dream aloud**. Your goal won't happen for you if you don't acknowledge it.

1. By stating your desire out loud you force your brain into action mode.
2. You also start building a support network.
3. If you want something, get off your ass—and go get it.

One of the first responsibilities I was given in the dining room was setting up and serving the Sunday brunch buffet. This being a country club, Sunday brunch was a fancy affair: white linen table cloths, silver serving dishes, some classical string music on the sound system...and then there was me, standing behind the eggs benedict table. Under my apron, I wore a concert tee from a recent Blue Oyster Cult and Black Sabbath show. They called the tour "Black and Blue"; it was fantastic. I remember the fancy dresses and suits of the members as they moved down the buffet line, choosing fruits and breads. The expression of one gentleman melted from eager anticipation to aversion as his gaze moved from the hollandaise sauce I was ladling on his dish to the name Black Sabbath on my shirt. He looked up at my long, permed, rocker hair, and then went to find a manager.

My work ethic was solid enough I wasn't formally reprimanded for this lapse in sartorial judgement. Just gently reminded, "Hey. You can't wear that to work." But I had already figured that out. I never wore that shirt at Wildwood again.

One of the more unexpected lessons I got from working in the country club dining room was the opportunity to unlearn some of my notions about rich people. I didn't realize going into it that I had a whole bunch of attitudes about the members, many of whom were business owners and self-made folks. It surprised me just how nice they were. Growing up, most people I knew, including some of my own family, claimed to hate rich people. They'd say things like, "They make money off the backs of the poor!" and "Money is the root of all evil." It was a clear us-versus-them idea of the way wealth worked.

I assumed the members would be nasty or looking to take advantage of me, but they were as nice as they could be. That experience of kindness and graciousness created a sort of whiplash that shattered my childhood beliefs. Looking back on it now, I

realize the way I was raised set up a false barrier to wealth. When they would say things like, "They're just out to screw us," a wall of suspicion, anger, and bitterness was erected between those country club members and me. My family made money seem like it was scarce and possibly dangerous. "What am I, made of money? Do you think money grows on trees?"

It makes me wonder, where do these beliefs come from? Do poor people they hate the rich because they're poor—or are they poor because they hate the rich?

When adults think about money that way, a part of them will always think they shouldn't try to get rich, because it will ruin them. I'm here to tell you that you can both have money and a kind heart. To be honest, wealth can be a source of great benevolence. It takes money to solve problems. With money, you can do more for the world than you can without it.

It has taken me a lifetime to unravel some of the barriers in my unconscious mind. I will talk in more depth about that in Chapter 9. For now, I will just say that we need to be more aware of where our judgements come from. They're not all helpful.

* * *

While Mr. Griff was a professional inspiration, one other figure in my life from Wildwood Country Club became a lifelong friend. When I first started washing dishes, there was an older guy there too. His name was Danny.

Danny was really skinny, and he had an odd-shaped face. His face was a little longer than normal, and he always looked a little tired. I knew something was up, but I wasn't sure what it was. I thought it would be best to get to know him a little bit before I asked him anything. One day, I went to him and I said, "All right, what's the story?"

He said, "Well, I have muscular dystrophy." The only thing I knew about muscular dystrophy was from Jerry's Kids: the ones on the telethon with wheelchairs and braces on their legs. But that didn't look at all like Danny. The man in front of me was in his early 20s; he walked and worked a regular job, but he apparently had a genetic disorder. Danny explained he had a variation of the disease called myotonic dystrophy. It meant that his muscles would slowly fail—including the muscles that enabled him to swallow—and his heart would eventually weaken and stop working, probably by age fifty.

Danny wasn't able to continue working for much longer after I met him at the country club, but we stayed friends. Once I started earning enough money to move out of my mom's house, I got a two-bedroom apartment and called up my friend. "Hey, Danny, how would you like to be my roommate?"

His monthly social security check helped a little bit with rent, but I mainly invited him to live with me because we had so much fun together. Plus, I knew how much he hated having to live with his parents. We had a hell of a time together, Danny and me. We liked to invite a bunch of our buddies over to play poker, drink beers, and get into shenanigans.

About the time my lease was up on that apartment, I realized Danny needed more than I could give him in the way of care. Just getting out of bed was hard for him, and I couldn't be around all the time. Danny was better off with his parents. Perhaps she understood Danny's frustration at being dependent, because his mom invited me to come live with them at their house to soften the blow of moving back home. I thought about it. They had plenty of room, and I enjoyed being around Danny.

"Okay," I said, "I'll absolutely come live with you guys."

MOTIVATION
BE GRATEFUL

I thought I had it rough growing up; then I met Danny. Watching him carry on, especially as his health deteriorated over the years, I learned to be grateful for my circumstances. I was blessed beyond belief to have a working pair of legs and the strength to use them.

In comparing my life to Danny's, I don't mean that I used my friend as an inspirational prop. I genuinely enjoyed having him in my life and spending time with him. I mean that feeling sorry for yourself is such a waste of time. It doesn't matter where you are in life, there will always be someone who has it harder than you. You can either spend time whining that it's harder for you than others—or you can start solving problems.

1. Be grateful for your abilities and blessings.
2. Look at what's going well and build on that.
3. Quit your damn crying.

CHAPTER 4

ON LEARNING HOW TO GET WHAT YOU WANT

AFTER I GRADUATED FROM HIGH SCHOOL, I SPENT A FEW MONTHS JUST GOING TO CONCERTS AND CAROUSING WITH FRIENDS AFTER SHIFTS AT WILDWOOD.

Though we were underage, we never had difficulty obtaining beer... just some difficulty enjoying it without getting picked up by the cops. It pissed me off to no end that they would confiscate my beer and drive me home to my mom's house. We were just punks who were killing time and trying to have fun, going to a lot of concerts. We saw all the great bands—The Stones, The Moody Blues, and Black Sabbath—of course. And I bought all the concert tees. In fact, that was my daily uniform: Chucks, Levi's, and a concert t-shirt.

Those were fun times, but it soon became apparent that lifestyle couldn't be my long-term plan. Busboy isn't a career goal; it's a stepping stone. It was time to figure out what I was going to be when I grew up.

I had an idea about that. My mom and my aunts were all hair stylists. It was practically the family business. Over the years, I saw that Mom had been able to keep food on the table and the car running on her single income, so I knew money could be made in the beauty industry. My Aunt Lena was an instructor in one of the local beauty schools, The School of Hair Design, so I thought, "I guess I'll try the hair thing." I applied for a little government grant to fund my $2,400 tuition to Lena's school and got it. I was all set.

It might seem weird for a straight, teenaged dude to set his sights on a career in a female-dominated industry, but it wasn't weird to me. I had already spent most of my life surrounded by the hair industry. Plus, I liked the company. When I walked in the first day (still wearing ratty jeans and a t-shirt), there were seventy girls and two guys.

"This will be just fine," I thought, liking my odds in the room.

I fell in love with doing hair right away. It gave me a way to utilize talents that I had, until then, taken for granted. I've always had a gift of gab, which I didn't really appreciate before then. I have always been adept at getting my way. Since styling is selling an idea about a person's self-image, explaining your vision and long-term plan to clients is a requirement of the job. I naturally had that going for me. Then I recognized the hand skills.

I was really good with my hands. It takes real dexterity to hold scissors correctly, while also manipulating the hair and a comb. Plus, there's an artistry to the job. You're taking a lump of clay and making it into a sculpture. Not everyone can do that. I realized, looking back, that I'd always had this skill. I had won some accolades in art classes over the years, but until everything clicked together in beauty school, I hadn't considered that ability especially usable.

At first, I wore my usual t-shirts and jeans every day. But the other students were showing up looking good, and I wanted to impress them. So, as I started to learn about style and fashion, off to TJ Maxx I went. I got a yellow banded-collar shirt, some pleated khaki pants, and a pair of boots with a little heel. The response was overwhelming.

"Oh my God, Bennie! Look at you! You look so good!"

Growing up, my family had despised the suit-wearing business people. It had just never occurred to me to wear anything similar. But when I wore my new, button-up shirt and nice-looking pants, I was treated differently. It was my first lesson on the power and importance of packaging and image.

NUTS & BOLTS
PACKAGING

Take it from a man who has spent a career in the beauty industry: image is crucial. Some people may try to convince you otherwise with slogans like, "Don't judge a book by its cover," or "Beauty is only skin deep." They miss the point. You can be the best salesperson in the world, but if you're wearing a Black Sabbath t-shirt selling Bibles (for example), your audience will have already shut you down before you open your mouth.

Packaging is what determines people's first impression of you. And that applies to the way you dress, the way you stand, and the way you smell. I know. You're thinking, "I know how to shower, Bennie." Hear me out.

Years after I had established a successful salon in Louisville, I came out to greet one of my regular clients. She had just been shampooed, and she looked unhappy. She turned to me and said, "Bennie, I'm not paying you the kind of money I pay you to come in here and smell cigarette smoke." The young man who had just shampooed her did so directly after a smoke break. When he leaned over her at the shampoo bowl, it ruined her entire experience.

Scent is paramount. It's emotional—and bad smells can kill relationships. Think about a time you visited a nasty, dirty gas station bathroom. The memory leaves a disgusted feeling behind, one that you can still tap into now. Don't ever leave your clients with a memory like that of you. Coffee breath, cigarette breath, or even burger breath shouldn't enter your clients' sphere. Mints are your friend. (Never gum—grazing animals belong in pastures.)

When you get ready to walk into the business place, think about how others perceive you.

What story are you telling with your body?

Let me illustrate the point. While driving in Louisville one day, I stopped at a light and noticed a gaggle of middle school girls crossing the street. They were cracking up and having fun together. The group was all about the same size, except for one girl. As they started walking across the street, they inadvertently fell into a single-file line. And I noticed the taller girl. She was probably ten inches taller than the others—a really striking young lady with very blond hair. While walking, she was slumping her shoulders with her back sloped downward—like she was doing everything she could not to be tall.

I saw her for less than twenty seconds from sixty feet away, and I got her whole story. Just by her posture, I could tell she felt self-conscious about being different and uncomfortable in her body. I wanted to shout at her, "Stand up straight and be proud!"

The way you carry yourself is part of your brand. Posture—how you walk in a room—must exude confidence. Especially in my industry, but for anyone trying to sell a service or product; clients want to feel like you are an expert in your field, like you've got the goods to take care of their needs. And if you walk like the above-mentioned young lady, or shake hands like a dead fish, they won't feel that confidence. As I like to say, "If you ain't got it, you can't give it."

You've got to be able to communicate with your customer. Whether you're doing hair or cleaning their dog's teeth, you're building a relationship with them. Bonding with customers comes from your energy, your stance, and your tone. Done well, you've converted a stranger to someone who looks forward to seeing you, who will come back to you because of their experience.

1. Consider the impression your clothing makes on people.
2. For God's sake, use mints after eating or drinking.
3. Stand up straight, be proud. If you don't, I'll bust your face.

Beauty school was going well. I was feeling proud of myself and starting to look and act like a professional when the most exciting opportunity caught my attention. My school was sending a team to a comb-out competition.

The National Cosmetology Association had sort of an Olympics for hairdressers. With just a comb, a good stylist can create a really arresting, artful look. In a comb-out competition, participants take a model backstage and set the hair on rollers or pin curls while judges watch. The judges then staple a net over the rollers so no one can touch the hair until the competition begins. Then, up on the big modeling stage, competitors line up and wait to hear the cue, "Remove your net." Off come the nets and out come all those curlers and pins. Then the announcers say, "Begin!" and competitors have ten minutes to create a masterpiece.

My school was really into this because the rival school in town was also very competitive in these events. And we wanted to win.

I had been in school about two months when the competition plans began. Usually only senior cosmetology students were allowed to participate, but because I was Lena's nephew, they let me try it.

There were about sixty students competing at the event. The day went well, I was pleased with my style, and I waited nervously as they announced all the winners. Third place was called. Then, second place was called, and my hopes rose...maybe it would be me! First place winner was...not me. I was pissed. But I saw the top ten list, and I was number seven.

"Well," I thought to myself, "I've been in school for two months, and I'm already ranked seventh in the state." I took it as a sign I was in the correct field.

Attending that competition opened up the world for me. As a kid, I just watched mom do her ladies to pay the bills. I had no idea hair could get me out of Louisville, much less to an international competition. I started looking around and seeing industry greats like Vidal Sassoon and the founder of Aveda, Horst Rechelbacher. These guys were world-class badasses—and they'd built empires. I started thinking maybe I could have a bigger life than had previously occurred to me.

The next fall, I was just about to graduate, and I tried the comb-out competition again. I got third place in the state of Kentucky that time. The improvement and continued status of top-tier achievement cemented my daydreams. That's when I realized, "Okay, I can really do something with hair." I was no longer the punk kid, getting delivered home by the local police (after they took all my beer).

I was a future magnate.

Before they'd even announced any winners on that second

competition, I got a job offer. There was a lady in the audience who had been watching me. She owned one of the top salons in the city at the time, Expressions Day Spa, and her daughter had been in beauty school with me. The daughter, Marion, came up to me while we were all waiting to hear the results. "Hey, my mom would like to talk to you."

"Okay," I said. That conversation with Marion's mom, Immy, changed my career path.

Immy was a Korean immigrant who had blasted onto Louisville's beauty scene. In no time flat, she had established one of the top salons in the city—and a tough-as-nails reputation as a dragon lady. Based on my reputation and my performance at last year's competition, Immy invited me to come apprentice for her after graduation.

On my first day with Immy, she showed me around the shop. In her broken English, she explained I would be sweeping floors, washing hair, doing laundry, and learning. And I would make twenty-five dollars a day.

"Great!" I thought. I didn't mind paying some dues. We all have to learn the ropes, right? Though I would eventually get sick of folding towels and prepping hair color for other stylists, I was pretty happy at first. The tips were great, I was surrounded by beautiful women all day, and I was learning how Immy ran her business, even though I didn't realize it at the time.

This was around 1983. The style at the time for men and women was long, permed, big hair, and getting bigger every year. Everyone wanted that, including me.

Immy would have a perm special every so often. Those days were nine or ten hours long. I was still apprenticing, so my job would be to take down the perm rods and rinse perm solution. At the end of one of those marathon days, Immy took the whole staff out to dinner at her favorite Korean place to say thank you.

Getting in her little Nissan, I remember she punched in the tape that was in the cassette player.

The voice that came on was deep with a thick Southern accent—thicker than mine even. He said, "People often say motivation doesn't last. Neither does bathing—that's why we recommend it daily." I was hooked. This motivational speaker was Zig Ziglar, one of the greats. Listening to Zig with Immy, I realized her success wasn't an accident. She was prospering because she was trying to be prosperous. Immy set out to learn and improve every day. I decided to adopt her habit and check out more of this Zig Ziglar guy, which led me to a lifetime of reading and listening to audio books from business writers and self-improvement writers.

One of the lessons from Zig that stuck with me long after that ride in Immy's car was this. **"You can have everything in life you want, if you will just help enough other people get what they want."**

"Ohhh," I thought.

I was starting to see that I really did want more from life than just a daily grind. I wanted to achieve, to be somebody important. I had always been a motivated kid. When a goal was set before me, I was like, "I don't care who I step on, I'm going." However, M&Ms and bell bottoms will only bring temporary happiness. Now I had the proper vehicle to help me grow, which was helping others. I learned to ask, "How can I help you get what you need? What can I do for you?"

In hairdressing, that need was making people look and feel great. I knew that if I could make them feel great, I was going to be rewarded both emotionally and financially. It was a beautiful epiphany.

MOTIVATION
PLAN—THEN DO IT

The only character development training I'd ever had in school was the sentence, "I think I can," from *The Little Engine that Could*.

Sure, trying hard and not giving up is a valuable lesson, but it's not the only thing you need to know in life. Learning about Zig Ziglar had a profound effect on me. Through his books and recordings, I discovered I could have more control over my circumstances than I had been led to believe. What Zig and many others taught me was: **you get what you think about**.

He also said, "The majority of people are 'wandering generalities' rather than 'meaningful specifics.' The fact is that you can't hit a target you can't see."

Zig was right.

You have to set goals to be successful. And, probably more importantly, you have to believe you can achieve them. Other people can sense when we believe in ourselves. If I went to an investor meeting slouching like that girl I saw walking across the street, trying to be shorter in order to fit in, I would be communicating the message, "This probably won't work out." When we coach our inner voices to be our own cheerleaders—that energy shows. And it effects others.

If you are sitting on a goal, listen to me. It takes guts to start a business, to walk away from a steady paycheck and go out on your own. If you own a flailing operation, I know it's paralyzing to restructure something that you know deep down is just not working. Too often, people dream of making the changes they know they should... they just don't ever do it. I don't want you to be one of those people lying in bed at night surrounded by the ghosts of opportunities saying, "We came to you."

These are the tools you need to swallow that fear and just freakin' go after it.

1. Seek out teachers who will encourage you to be your best.
2. Set goals.
3. Believe that you can achieve.

I hadn't been with Immy for my full year of apprenticeship when I jumped ship. I thought I knew everything I needed to know, and I was still stuck folding her towels. I went to work for a salon that was owned by a modeling agency. This was a small-town operation; however, I think everyone wanted to go to Milan and Paris. My education and metamorphosis continued in this new environment.

The modeling agency had an education arm, with classes such as hair care and makeup technique, as well as runway walking classes. The owner who hired me to cut hair asked me to come in to discuss possible commissions for sending clients her way. She was such a good salesperson; she had me signed up for $800 worth of classes so fast, it made my head swim. I walked into the conversation thinking I would be getting more money—and ended up paying her a week's salary!

"What just happened?" I wondered.

In the end, taking those classes buffed my new-found sense of style to a polished finish. The teacher of the guy's classes taught us how to walk, how to dress, and how to speak...it was a killer education. And it opened me up completely to fashion. T.J. Maxx started my obsession with clothing; this completed it. Within eighteen months, I went from concert t's and Chuck Taylors to leather jackets with studs. Basically, if it was on MTV in 1984, I was wearing it with relish.

After I finished my classes, I recognized there was an opportunity to teach there. I signed up to teach for two reasons: I knew I should work on my public speaking, and the gig paid fifty dollars. Every other Wednesday evening, a group of thirteen and fourteen-year-old girls would come to the class where I taught proper hair care and styling. I didn't really know much beyond the basics—I was barely eighteen months past my beauty school graduation—but they didn't know that.

The other stylists in that salon had grown jaded about those classes. "I don't want to deal with that," they'd say. So, they were shocked and a little jealous when I surpassed them in clientele. I went from having nothing to do at the salon all day to being the busiest guy in the place—all because those girls and their mothers decided to give me a try after watching my shampoo speech.

That success led to an invitation to do hair for the modeling agency's photo shoots. Every year, this agency would put out a catalog of their models' head shots. From babies up to elderly people, they published a book of everyone available to do small modeling jobs in the Ohio River Valley. For eighteen bucks a head, I styled model after model, up to twenty in a row, all day long. We did that in Louisville, then Indianapolis, then Cincinnati. It was really exciting to see a full look come together with hair, makeup, and photography. Seeing the headshots so soon after I had done the work really helped me develop my eye. I learned balance and proportion in design. For instance, a small change in someone's bang length could change their whole appearance. Because of that,

I got really good, really fast at being able to envision my work beforehand, which has helped me tremendously as a high-end stylist. My eye, plus my communications skills, were the building blocks that led me to real money in the styling world.

Looking back, I can see the connecting thread that led to early success. I didn't know at the time that signing up to teach a bunch of middle schoolers would get me polished skills and into modeling shoots. I just said yes when an opportunity presented itself. I learned from that experience that communication is a prerequisite for success.

All that success was exciting, but it still wasn't enough for me. I wanted out of my podunk hometown. I was twenty-one, pretty full of myself, and dying for the excitement of a big city. My idea of glamour and sex appeal was *Miami Vice*, the hottest show at the time. My aunt Lena had moved to Florida, where she was working as a cosmetology instructor; I figured she could help me get a job there. So, I bought some loafers and threw out my socks. I was Miami bound!

CHAPTER 5

"BIG TIME"

MIAMI WAS A CRAZY PLACE TO BE IN THE MID-1980S. IT WAS EXCITING, WILD, GLAMOROUS— AND A LITTLE BIT DANGEROUS. I WAS DYING TO LIVE THERE.

My introduction to all this mayhem was *Miami Vice*. I absolutely worshipped it. The money—the girls—the glamour—were all intoxicating. It was rumble-tumble, rock 'em-sock 'em robots. The flash and adrenaline of this big city were the exact opposite of Bullitt County. So, at age twenty-one, I left Kentucky and moved to Florida. I got an apartment right in the center of the action— Coconut Grove. I didn't know jack shit about anything; it was great. For me, it was like going off to college: an education about life and what it was like to be my own person. Miami grew me up substantially. I might've been a little homesick, but not for long. The culture, the food, and the music were all eye opening. Living in Miami gave me a bachelor's degree in life.

I had a place to live; next, I needed a job. Fortunately, I'm in an industry with zero unemployment. A lot of people don't know that about the hair business. Too often, the industry is a punchline, the butt of the perpetual joke. From the song "Beauty School Drop Out" to the movie *Shampoo* to Marisa Tomei's unemployed hairdresser role in *My Cousin Vinny*, the media portrays me and my colleagues as poor, dumb, and lazy.

I'm here to tell you it's just not the case. If you want a job as a hairdresser, you can find one. Hair is recession proof, and if you know what you're doing, it's a serious money maker. Those working at a swank, well-run hair salon are often the primary earners in their family. It's possible to do over $100,000 per year in hair these days, if you've got the skills and the attitude in place. By the way, those same lessons of business acumen and positive thinking apply to most any small business. Throughout this book, I'll show you how.

Finding a job wasn't hard. I was aiming for the *right* job. I ticked down the yellow page listings for South Beach salons, which was where I wanted to work. When I called, I did not ask, "Do you have any openings?"

I asked, "How much are your haircuts?" click.

"How much are your haircuts?" click.

"How much are your haircuts?"

When I heard "treinta y cinco" (thirty-five dollars), I was in!

NUTS & BOLTS
AIM AT YOUR TARGETS

One of my goals in Miami was to make bank. So, I wasn't just looking for any job; I was looking for the highest paying gig I could find. That's why I learned which part of Miami was the most affluent and called all the salons in that area. I needed to know who was charging what. I didn't want to work at a mid-level or a bargain place. I wanted the clients who had money to spend.

It's a good thing I did. Back in Louisville, my haircuts were sixteen dollars per cut—and that had been considered high for the market. My mom was still charging eight dollars at the time. She thought I was nuts to ask thirty-five dollars. "Nobody's going to pay that much," she told me.

I said, "Mom, they already are." If I hadn't done my research, I might have just carried on charging half the potential Miami rate and left all that profit on the table.

My point is, you must aim at targets if you want to grow. Don't just land at any job—create your perfect job. Do your homework and learn as much as you can about the situation or person to understand how to position yourself.

To aim correctly you need to know what your goal is. Is it more money? Opportunities to advance? Solid leadership? What's the prize you'll be grabbing?

1. Form goals.
2. Position yourself in places that make your goals attainable.
3. Never let naysayers talk you out of taking big steps.

I interviewed with Ugo, the owner of Ugo di Roma in the Omni Mall (a major player at the time) and got the job immediately. The salon was in the heart of downtown Miami and served the upscale, Cuban clientele of mostly second-generation businesswomen or businessmen's wives. They had money and did not mind spending it on their hair.

The one catch? Spanish was the predominant language spoken. I didn't always understand what they were asking me. So, I hustled to learn a little beauty-related Spanish and worked extra hard to make sure my clients were happy. They and the other stylists all took me in like family. I loved it.

Then there was Ugo. Watching my boss work was something special. While the rest of us were using curling irons, Ugo would pull out an arsenal of round brushes and go to work straightening all that curly Afro-Cuban hair into the smooth, voluminous styles that were popular at the time. (People with curly hair always want their hair smooth; people with smooth hair always want it to be curly.) It was like magic.

"Damn, he's good," I would say as I watched closely. That's where I learned my round-brushing technique. Actually, Ugo's salon gave me the opportunity to learn many things: language, technique, and methods for working with different hair textures.

After working in Miami for a year or so, I had built a nice clientele. I was busy every day, all day, something that usually takes a few years to achieve. I remember Ugo coming in and saying, "Good grief, son, what are you doing?"

"I'm gonna be the best there is, dude," I said.

He smiled. "I like to hear stuff like that."

Because Ugo owned two salons, he wasn't onsite very much, and it bugged me. I couldn't have explained why at the time. Looking back on it, I now know I was dissatisfied with the lack of leadership. I loved learning about the business and new techniques, but I wanted to work for a serious businessperson. I didn't know that's what I was looking for. If I had, I could have aimed for it.

Instead, I found myself job hopping at the rate of about one salon per year. In every place—Louisville, Fort Lauderdale, Boca Raton, and Miami—I was quick to gain clients and quick to grow disillusioned. High-end salons have the benefit of excellent paychecks plus tips. However, without any structure and a good system in place, and a drama-fueled boss on top of it, it's just not worth the effort to work there.

In every new location, I would look for the advancement I had been promised in the interview. The owners spun dreams of

stage work, photo shoots, and artistic teams to reel me in. They never appeared. These salon owners were all just hustling to cover the next payroll or electric bill. Maybe they hoped to work up to those next-level skills, but they didn't seem to be able to make the time. They were just spinning their wheels every day, cutting hair furiously, and putting out the fires that they had themselves set. One extreme example I can share is a salon owner who actually got arrested for breaking into his own businesses and stealing the stereo equipment—to sell it for crack.

I can see this pattern now in retrospect. Nine salons in nine years is too many. I know now that it's not the location, but the mentality, that makes success. I needed to be my own leader. At the time, I kept chasing the wisps of my dreams. "Maybe the next place will be better," I kept thinking...which is how I found myself working at the Fort Lauderdale Saks Fifth Avenue Salon.

One day, a friend told me about a girl working in the skincare department. He said she was beautiful and interesting. "Send her up, and I'll cut her hair for her."

Maria was her name. She was from Sweden and had decided to go see the world, starting with Florida. She managed one of the beauty product lines at Saks Fifth Avenue. She was assertive and interesting. I wanted to know more about her. I asked her out. Six months later, we tied the knot—and the rest is history. We've been married for over thirty years now.

MOTIVATION
A WORD ABOUT COURAGE

It doesn't matter what type of small business you own (or hope to own). One quality you must cultivate is courage. That may sound like tired advice to you. It may be tired advice. But, in my opinion, old principles wouldn't have lived so long if they weren't true.

It takes courage to make a big jump, whether that's relocating to a new city, trying out a different career, or just taking the next step with your existing job. If you don't have enough courage and willingness to take some sort of risk, whether measured or otherwise, you're doomed to a life of mediocrity.

When I moved to Miami, I was picking a target. You know, the new city was the wild animal. I wasn't shot gunning. I was targeting with a .30-06. I moved there specifically because I knew there was money to be made in that market.

I know that for some of you, there's a lot of fear keeping you from pulling the trigger. I hope this book will help build your confidence. You control your destiny simply through the way you think about your goals. To paraphrase Gandhi: Belief becomes thoughts, which become ideas, which become actions. Believe in your core that you *can* succeed, and you will. Aim for your targets. Then pull the trigger.

1. The oft-repeated aphorisms are true. Respect them.
2. Again–pick your targets.
3. Gain some courage and take the leap.

While it's true that I was too flighty for my own good in Florida, one thing I did do right was learn to market myself. When I would leave a salon for another in the same city, I wanted to take my clientele with me. So, I hired a writer—basically a PR person—to help create a package I could send out to all of my customers. It had a nice photograph and some great copy.

This was 1986, before the concept of branding was part of my thinking—and long before people curated their personal brands on social media. I don't know how I even thought to do it; I was maybe twenty-four-years-old. I can't believe it occurred to me, but instinctively (in my gut), I knew it was right; I just knew I had to do it that way. I include this example to illustrate two points. One, trust your gut. I have a lot of faith in intuition; it's the only reason I'm where I am in life. Cultivate your intuition, and let it influence your decisions. Two, don't be afraid to hire professional services. Some might say the decision to fork over a chunk of cash for a highly polished package was a stupid decision. I was "just a hairdresser" and a young one at that. I reject the entire paradigm that opinion is based upon.

Most people limit how far they can advance by their attitudes toward money. They build their lifestyle around XYZ amount of money, say $500 a week. Their budget is so tightly oriented around that number that it never occurs to them to make more. The possibility there's more money out there, waiting for somebody to grab, doesn't even enter their consideration. The number one reason most people aren't wealthy is 'cause it never freakin' occurred to them to become wealthy. People's families and upbringing have a strong influence on their relationship to money. "Well, Dad made $60,000 a year at the steel mill. That's good money," they'll tell me.

"Good money?" I say. "Are you insane!" I tell people sometimes, "If you think fifty dollars is expensive, you're never gonna have more than fifty dollars."

My point is, you can change the way you look at money and the costs required to operate on the level you're aiming for. If I flinch at a $5,000 invoice for a new website, I'm never going to have more than $5,000. Those services are worth it. It saves me from spending twice as long trying to do it myself (badly), and the target market I'm aiming at will respect the professional image I present. And they will pay more for it.

Let's say that marketing package cost me $1,200 in 1986. That money paid to a writer and designer earns me another 100 new customers who are going to spend an average of $1,000 a year with me. Was that $1,200 a smart investment? Of course it was. Could I have gotten that caliber of paying client with a shitty clip-art flyer I did myself at Kinko's? Hell, no.

* * *

Due to my gift of gab, I could pull together a loyal client base in every city I moved to in Florida. But the pattern started to wear on me. Get a job; build a solid base; watch the owners devolve in drama and dumb-fuckery; quit; repeat. When that last crack-addled salon owner went to jail, I threw up my hands in disgust. "Fuck this business," I said to Maria. "Every salon owner is nuts. This is crazy shit. I'm out!"

I hung up my scissors and quit the hair business. Maria and I moved back to Louisville to find some other way of living.

CHAPTER 6

TRYING, FAILING, THEN TRYING AGAIN

MARIA AND I MOVED BACK TO LOUISVILLE AND RENTED A CHEAP APARTMENT. SHE GOT A JOB WAITING TABLES, WHILE SHE STUDIED TO GET HER REALTOR'S LICENSE AT NIGHT.

I was adamant about not doing hair, besides an occasional trim for friends on my back porch. I was ready to try something totally different. I thought I might be good at flipping houses; however, you need capital to invest in real estate. I was twenty-four and broke. My years in hair had been exciting and educational. I made great money but lacked the business acumen to manage it well. My financial savvy was zip. As far as savings go, I was starting from scratch.

Luckily, I'm a gifted gabber. I became pals with my landlord, an up-and-coming real estate investor named Walt Jones. I asked if he had any jobs, and he immediately put me to work painting walls in some houses he was flipping. I dug in, like I usually do, and cranked out the job quickly.

"Good God!" he said.

I was like, "Of course. I don't mess around. Let's get this shit done."

That partnership worked out well. We're still good friends, in fact. I provided labor for Walt—drywall and painting—stuff like that. Walt also helped me pay for real estate school. Then I worked as an agent out of Walt's office, putting together deals on commercial properties and finding houses we could flip or turn into rentals.

I remember my first deal was a beautiful thing. I searched expired listings, properties that had been for sale but expired before there were any takers. I called all those owners and found one guy who was thrilled to get my call. He was selling a thirty-six-unit apartment building for $550,000. When I asked if he still wanted to sell, he said, "Oh my God, yes! I'm stuck handling it, and we gotta get rid of the thing."

I said I was interested in listing it and might have some investors for him.

Walt and I worked out a deal. Essentially it was a contract saying that if I sold the property, I would get paid. Walt, for his part, agreed to show the building to some of his investors. If any of them were interested, he would split the 10% commission with me. After about five months, we had all the money lined up, the deal went through, and my buddy and I earned $50,000.

Slick! I thought.

My chunk of that money went straight into my first house flip. I got a duplex, fixed it up, sold it for a profit, and repeated that pattern for about a year. I enjoyed going into the older neighborhoods and finding beautiful Victorian houses that were down on their luck. They were split into duplexes, and many had become pretty run down. I would get in there and replace the old fixtures, floors, and cabinets—and paint everything else. Every day, I mucked around in jeans and t-shirts. I was painting, drywalling, and doing demolition—whatever needed doing that didn't need a licensed expert. I was feeling proud of the fruits of my labor; however, I was getting tired of being covered in gunk all day, every day. I enjoyed seeing the houses shine, but—alone in those houses—I found I really missed the cool factor of the hair business and the lively salon life. It was late 1990, and I wanted to get back to a world with some flash and pop.

It was time to get back into hair.

* * *

Though I was in my hometown—turf I knew well—I used my Miami trick to get the best-paying gig. I called around to find the most expensive salon and got a job there. That gig lasted about two months before I recognized the same missing ingredient that most of my other jobs had lacked. No freakin' leadership. Again! I left and went back to Immy's salon.

It was nice to be back where everything started. Kind of like returning to your old high school, everything seemed smaller and less intimidating than it was just a few years before.

One day, I was thumbing through an industry magazine. An ad caught my eye, "Have you ever thought about being a platform artist and doing stage work?"

Yes. Yes, I have, I thought to myself.

One of the things that rocks about the beauty industry is that it always pushes the artistic envelope. When we get together at conferences, we love to show off and share new ideas. The general public never really hears about our hair shows, but these events are part education, part motivation, and part entertainment. Hair shows are where hair and beauty trends are born and where platform artists go to shine. On stage, a platform artist demonstrates product, technique, and the newest looks. It's their job to get a group of stylists excited about our industry.

The ad I saw was looking for stylists to try out for a team that would represent the US on a hair tour. The team of four would be called American Team Yes (for youth, energy, and style). Sitting in the salon, looking at the magazine, I imagined myself on stage again. Applause, admiration, and excitement...I wanted in.

I made my audition tape, with help from a local PR firm, and I got the spot. I was one of four people who would represent the youth of American style at trade shows across north America, starting in New York. It was March 1992.

You've probably never heard of any of these shows, but let me tell you, this was a big deal. I was twenty-seven and invited to perform on the same stage with the industry's top talent. I would be seen by everyone who was anyone in my industry, and I would get to observe the top talent from the other international teams from France, Japan, Germany, and Argentina. The learning opportunity alone was invaluable. We performed in New York, Seattle, Dallas, Toronto, and Miami. Some of the stylists clearly enjoyed the attention and got big heads. Inevitably, they pissed people off. Others just did the work, and then went back home, end of story. Then there were a couple of team members, over the life of the program, who went on to exciting things.

As I went through that tour, I asked myself this question: *How can I parlay this incredible experience into something bigger? Sure, this is cool, but what's next?*

I decided the next thing for me was to be my own boss. I was weary of the lack of leadership in my industry. All the pageantry around the Team YES tour had an energy that I just knew could be used to power something else.

So, I put together a video tape of my stage shows and started showing it to possible investors in Louisville. Walt, my real estate buddy, and his mother, Wanda, were interested. They had sourced a couple of really cool properties close to downtown Louisville: old shotgun houses in a neighborhood that had the potential to become a salon space. I sat down with them, popped my tape in the VCR, and told them to check it out. I did the same with another investor, Kim.

"I'm going to show you what I've been doing. This is the other side of the industry."

Kim said, "Damn it, Bennie! I didn't know you were into that!"

I explained my vision of owning my own salon to Kim and said, "I have a little money, but I need investors." She wrote me a check right then; I think it was for $6,000 or $7,000. Another investor did the same thing, and I was ready to look for locations.

NUTS & BOLTS
PARLAY YOUR SUCCESS

The tour I was on, Team YES, continued that same pattern for ten years. Select four team members, tour the US, and that's it. I'm not sure what happened to the other partici-pants, or if they achieved any greater level of success after the team. I'm sure some did. But I'm not sure how many of them recognized a true opportunity.
I sure did.

I wasn't going to be satisfied with just being on the team. I wanted more. I saw that tour as a launching pad. So often, people have a success, but they miss that it's an opportunity. The lesson here is: **Think very seriously about how to parlay your experiences into more**. How can you get the most out of a particular situation? How can you magnify one win into more wins? It's like a basketball game, when the thrill of a three-pointer energizes the team, and then they go score a few more while the other team lags further behind. Why? It's a momentum thing.

After that, I went home and put together a salon invest-
ment deal. I have no idea if the thirty-nine other people
did that or not. They might not have known they could.
Some people weren't prepared for what could happen
for them. They didn't even know how to **think about** what
could happen for them. They thought the tour was the
peak of their excitement. For me, it was barely scratching
the surface of possibility.

1. Believe that you can have more—that you deserve more.
2. Dream big.
3. When one success happens think, "How can I turn this
   into more success?"

While I was gathering investors, I was also building my reputation
in the region. Louisville culture is built around whiskey, horses,
and baseball bats: the Louisville Sluggers. Most news coverage
centers around those three main things. Fashion or beauty might
tiptoe into the style section of the newspaper during Kentucky
Derby season, but that's about it. So, there was tremendous opportunity for some fresh coverage when I got onto Team YES. The
same PR representative who had helped me make the audition
tape pitched all the local media outlets with press releases and story suggestions about this stratospheric success from a Louisville
native.

They bit hard. I had newspaper stories, business papers fea-
tures, city magazine stories, and TV spots all trumpeting a variation on the theme, "Local Boy Does Good!"

My clientele grew like crazy, and I sensed the moment had
come.

When I started to be too popular to keep up with my regular
clients, I knew it was time to pull the trigger on my own salon.

Hair by Bennie and Friends opened on Frankfort Avenue in 1992. My real estate experience really helped spearhead that venture, because I had a good sense of where to place it and what it should look like. Plus, Walt, his mom, and I were already investing in these really old, run-down homes for little money. The house my salon opened in was actually one of three side-by-side shotgun houses in a questionable area of Louisville. Walt bought it, stripped it down to the studs, and rebuilt it as a salon. I helped with the labor and then leased it from him.

Because the PR coverage continued to bring new clients, the day Hair by Bennie and Friends opened, we were already close to capacity. It was me, a front desk person, and another hairdresser. Within a month, I hired a third hairdresser. Within ninety days, we needed to expand to the house next door.

I'll admit here that I started making mistakes as a boss. For example, one of the hairdressers I hired was an established stylist who I lured away from another salon. I'm ashamed of that and will never steal someone else's employee again. Also, I expanded too quickly.

Let me explain.

Within my first year of business ownership, I had nine stylists working in about 2,000 square feet of salon space. My flagship salon had been expanded to the house next door via a hallway. We were crazy busy, yet the profits never appeared. I approached my pay structure as an employee, meaning I paid my hairdressers what I wanted to be paid, which—it turns out—hurt the business. The stylists were on a sliding commission split; they were making bank from all the customers my PR campaign was drawing in, and I was barely even drawing a salary after expenses. I owned the most popular salon in town and was cutting hair like a demon every day—and yet we barely had grocery money at home. I couldn't understand what I was doing wrong.

Looking back now, I can see that I should have schooled myself on the financials before ever hiring an employee. If I had it to do over, here's what I would suggest to the younger me:

> Prepare yourself before you pull the trigger. I do believe in the ready, shoot, aim philosophy. However, make sure your foundation is rock solid first. By that, I mean seek the correct skill set. Financials first! If you get your initial financial structure set coming out of the gate, you can slowly learn some of the other leadership essentials. You can't learn financials after the fact, because you won't survive long enough to get it right. You will have to start over.

You need someone who knows and understands the industry you're wanting to play in. Find an experienced owner and ask these questions about profit and loss:

Where should your supply costs live?

Where should your labor costs be?

What kind of percentage should your rent be in relationship to revenue?

If you can get a grip around some of that up front, you can learn other leadership skills as you go. The only reason my salon was able to survive those first few precarious years was because my business volume behind the chair was so high. Little did I know; the chaos was just beginning.

* * *

To keep a toe in the edgy art-side of my industry, I regularly did photo shoots. I wanted to keep the creative juices flowing and didn't want to lose the eye I had developed cutting hair for model shoots. So, I brought in the same photographer I met at the modeling agency all those years ago and went crazy on models a couple of times a year. When we had a solid collection of looks, I submitted those shots to the various trade publications like *Modern Salon, American Salon,* and *Studio Salon.* At the time, those trade magazines were always looking for high-end photography to feature. They welcomed the submissions and ran many of them under the salon's name.

Partly because of that name recognition, we won salon of the year in the 1994 Modern Salon's Annual Competition. That competition has morphed into the Salon Today, Top 200. Our design aesthetic was something special—it still is. We had vaulted ceilings and badass light fixtures...cool shit, top to bottom. Our trophy shelf was starting to fill up and, though the money was still a problem, I was really proud of what we were building.

One day, in 1996, I was home sick with the flu. It was a rare day off for me when the phone rang. The lady on the other end said, "Hi, my name is so and so. I'm with *Glamour* magazine."

I said, "Hmm, okay."

"Well, we're doing an article about the top salons all throughout the United States and your name has come up."

If I remember correctly, I asked her, "Well, how did you find me?"

She explained, "Well, when we do these kinds of pieces, we call the industry magazines and see who are the players in these various markets, because we're exposed primarily to New York and LA."

"Oh, very interesting," I said as my heart rate cranked up a bit.

"Your name came up repeatedly for the Ohio Valley area. We'd like to put you in our magazine."

I said, "Well, of course."

The day that feature came out, I was so excited. Hair by Bennie and Friends was seen by millions of *Glamour* magazine readers. It should have been the most exciting thing that ever happened to me, and it was...until it tanked everything. That *Glamour* feature was the final crack in our already weak business model. It caused a massive meltdown in my salon.

MOTIVATION
NO MODESTY!

New business owners (or those thinking about a new business) have to avoid a whole bunch of pitfalls. One that I'd advise you to throw right out the window is apprehension about marketing yourself. People think they're being humble, to which I say bullshit. You're robbing the world of your greatness. Get out there and show it off!

Always enter contests, say yes when speaking offers arrive, and give product away as you're getting known. And when your greatness gets recognized? Shout about it. Keep numbers on it. Collect those awards and recognitions, then hire a public relations consultant to spread the good news. Send an announcement to your newspaper; use it in your marketing. The entire concept behind this book is how to think bigger. Being shameless about your particular expertise is a part of that. Go get your chunk of the market and be proud!

The only caution I want to stress with regard to marketing yourself is **be prepared** before you announce yourself to the world. As you're about to read, the biggest promotional coverage I ever got just about drove me out of business.

1. Get your ducks in a row, business-wise. Then go forth and prosper.
2. There is no such thing as bragging in business. If you've got something special, then tell people.
3. Hire marketing help to make the most of your awards or accomplishments.

By the time Hair by Bennie and Friends was in a national magazine, I had expanded to yet another building next door. There were 3,800 square feet, a staff size between twenty-five and thirty, two front desk people, and a bunch of apprentices—and we were just about to break one million dollars in annual sales.

Everything looked amazing from the outside. The truth was, we were a mess internally. Ironically, the problems I was seeing in my salon were the same types of drama-driven scenes I used to run from. I just didn't have the leadership chops that I needed. I thought I was being a good boss and building my staff correctly, but I really wasn't.

All but two employees were people I had plucked from beauty school and trained up as assistants, who became full stylists. I still believe in that model. Train people correctly from the start. That way they learn your philosophy and practices, and they don't have to unlearn bad habits. That approach works really well when your standard business practices are consistent and documented. I know that now; I didn't back then.

These days there's a script for every single client interaction that happens under my roof. For example, we answer the phone exactly the same way every time, "Thank you for choosing Nova Salon, where we love every hair on your head. My name's Bennie. How may I assist you?"

I'll get more into the nuts and bolts of my specific practices in a later chapter, but I share that practice now to illustrate what a mess things were in the early 90's.

No one answered the phone the way I wanted them to. My people just did what they wanted. There wasn't consistency across the staff, and no one ever told them no. I've come to realize that talented people want strong leadership. Because I was trying to be both a co-worker, a friend, and a boss, I was wearing too many hats and terrible at all of them—especially leadership. Because of my lack of business acumen and leadership skills, I lost my entire staff, which equaled almost a million dollars' worth of revenue a year.

* * *

Along with my profits, I said goodbye to the hairdressers who left. I know now that everything that happened with them was **all my fault**. They were wonderful, creative people, and I didn't do my job. Had I been a better leader for them, they probably wouldn't have left.

At the time the walk-out happened, I hated my business. It felt as though it was sucking the life out of me. I can see now that I wasn't even close to prepared for being a boss. I wasn't ready for that type of exponential growth; the finances weren't in line. I had no systems built to handle that kind of traffic. Often in business, you'll find owners who tend to blame their employees like I did. Think of complaints about someone's staff as a red flag. This is a tell-tale sign the owner is passing the buck and refusing to be a leader.

I once heard a saying that rang true for me. "Be careful, because you can market your ass right out of business." The *Glamour* feature was intended as a boost to business, but those new clients overwhelmed what already wasn't working. Though I would still say yes to *Glamour* again if I had it to do over, I can see now that I hadn't prepared my business for the kind of exposure I was generating.

Completely sick of running my business, I decided to turn it into a chair rental salon. I thought I would no longer have to manage employees, only to discover that I still had the responsibility for the overhead of the business. The only income I would receive was what I made working behind the chair, which is not why I started the business in the first place. I ran things that way for about a year only to realize I had zero control of my business, because I was the landlord, not the employer. I could not mandate the hours, the dress code, the dialogue, or anything else for the hairdressers.

It took me some time and a hard gut check before I was ready to recognize that I hadn't really been in business all this time. I was acting like I was just a solo hairdresser, not a business owner. I want to be clear about this: I'm not saying chair rental was the right model or the wrong model. I'm saying chair rental wasn't for me, and I had to find that out the hard way. Whatever business you're in, look at the different models available and make sure you choose the one that's right for you.

CHAPTER 7

RUN THE BUSINESS OR THE BUSINESS RUNS YOU

MY SALON'S REPUTATION WAS SUFFERING; I STILL HATED MY BUSINESS; IT WAS TIME TO TRY YET ANOTHER SOLUTION TO MY LEADERSHIP PROBLEMS.

I sat them all down and I said, "Okay, here's what I'm going to do, y'all. I'm going back to employee-based pay; I'm going to do commission. Here's how we're going to answer the phone; here's how we're going to dress; here's where you're going to be and when. This is how things are going to be at my salon now."

It was a total restructuring, top to bottom. All but two people left. They were all good folks, and I was sorry to see them go. I've got people working for me now making $150,000 per year. That income is based completely on our booking procedures. The high earners are never slow; it's very difficult to get an appointment.

That restructure was about taking control of my business. Essentially, I had a rebirth. I recognized there was a right way to treat the customers. I knew what a professional environment looked like and how it ran. We had been missing the mark—by a lot. I also knew how much money I wanted to make and how much money I wanted my people to make. I said to myself, "Even if I have to cut hair by myself, this is the way it has to be."

* * *

This re-boot started in the year 2001. It was a new millennium. I had a new attitude, a new set of business practices, and two employees—in 3,800 square feet of salon space.

It's funny to think back on that time now. The place was a cavern without all those hairdressers. Most days it was me and nineteen empty chairs. My clients would come in and ask, "Where is everybody?"

I would say, "Ah, it's the calm before the storm." That was my a.m. phrase.

Then, of course, my p.m. phrase was, "Oh man, you should have seen it earlier."

NUTS & BOLTS
DON'T BE HELD HOSTAGE

When I first opened my salon, I was afraid to be the boss. I made the mistake of thinking that everyone was like me: they would show up and work hard. Instead I discovered that some people are motivated and some people are not.

There was no leadership, just like in the nine salons I had quit. I learned the hard way that compromising my standards just made everyone unhappy, and the salon lost money. The minute I made the decision to follow through, the salon turned around. After seven years of owning a salon, I was finally in business for real.

1. Never hold yourself hostage.
2. Never compromise your standards.
3. Be the boss.

A lot of folks will venture into business, but never truly decide to be *in* business. That was me too. I was in business for seven years before I finally made the decision to be *in* business. What does that mean?

Well, we all daydream about what our future business will look like or how fantastic it will be to work for ourselves. I can tell you from hard experience that it takes more than being good at your profession to be a successful business owner. When you fly solo, like I did renting chairs in other people's shops, you only need customer skills and individual money sense. Once you take on employees, you must have control of your staff and your finances.

To be the boss, you've got to be able to say, "Here's how we're going to do it. This is it: no compromises, no second guessing. We're solid on this plan. Full steam ahead."

In addition, to be profitable, **you must understand profit & loss statements**. That lack of knowledge is tragically common among small business owners. You don't need to be a freakin' CPA, but—first and foremost—you have to understand where your money is and where it's going. I didn't pay attention to that out of the gate, and it hurt me. We were great at making money, but we didn't have any idea how to control it, which is why it took so long to become profitable. Bottom line, in order to have control, you have to make the decision to **be in business**.

When all twenty-one stylists quit, I was happy and sad to see them go. I liked them as people, but I was glad to be starting over. Quite frankly, I messed up with them. It's much easier to set protocol correctly from the beginning of employment than to change everything in the middle. You can't put the toothpaste back in the tube.

I started hiring exclusively from beauty schools. If somebody knocked on my door saying, "Hey, I've got a clientele of $200,000 a year, can I work here?" I said no. It was difficult to do that; however, I knew that if I had any chance of getting employees to follow my standard practices, they had to be free of other systems and habits.

You may do things differently and hire employees with experience. That's fine. The point I'm making here is that you, as the boss, need to make sure your systems and business practices are run the way you want them to be. Write down the best practices for your industry and require employees to adhere your standards.

When I had to hire so many new people at once, it was hard. My new staff members were young and unsure of their career paths. I had to learn that that's okay. When you hire kids, they don't always know up front if this is the job for them. We went through beauty school grads like water. We'd hire three or four, one might stay. Hire two, both of them would leave, and so on. With the benefit of seventeen years of hindsight, I would still make the decision to hire only new grads.

My way has resulted in some rock star employees. Plus, with the benefit of a group of experienced staff to keep the wheels rolling, new kids join right in with enthusiasm. Though our beginning years were tiring, those young people have been a Godsend.

MILLENNIALS ROCK

Some employers my age have developed the wrong idea about 20-plus-somethings. They call them lazy, entitled millennials. To that, I say bullshit. The same people who are reluctant to hire young people are the ones who have no leadership skills. They have trouble with youth because they haven't decided to be the boss. I think every person has value, no matter what.

That value simply needs to be nourished. As a boss, you must encourage your employees and care for their value. Hold your people accountable and assume they're capable of achieving all goals unless they prove otherwise.

Remembering what Zig Ziglar taught me, I find that the more kids I can help carve out the correct career, the better my career is going to be. Sometimes the kids will stay with me, sometimes they won't. Either way, I know they've got the right foundation to grow. I'm encouraging the next generation.

Organizations who refuse to include and encourage younger members do so at their own peril. We've all seen those businesses whose clients were the peers of the owner. As the owner ages, so do the clients. Profits decline as the base moves away or dies. That's not going to happen to my salon. My long-term clients are still there, however **they're not the only ones**, and that's key. My millennial staff keep me on my toes. They're better at spotting trends, thus they're preserving this fifty-ish guy's relevance. They keep my salon youthful.

You may be asking yourself, so what? I don't own a salon. How does this apply to me? If you own any type of small business— say a dental practice, a welding shop, or any type of professional service—the lesson remains. No matter your type of business**, always be recruiting**. Remember, however, fresh graduates have education but no experience. They know theory; they don't know standard practices. As a boss, it's your responsibility to help them learn those. More than that, you need to **help them dream**.

The number one problem in small businesses is poor leadership. One symptom of that missing ingredient is the lack of a standardized training program. Asking the girl at the front desk to show the new kid the ropes doesn't cut it. Employees can't be held accountable if your processes aren't documented. Write down the best practices; script your phone greeting and any other key customer interactions so employees understand exactly what is expected of them. Have a detailed training agenda, one with vision. Show your new recruits how year one looks. Show them how year two looks. "Here's what's possible in year three and four," and so on.

If I own ABC Labs and I hire someone with a master's degree in biology, I can't assume this twenty-four-year-old knows what to stretch for. It's my job to teach them the ropes, but also to inspire them to keep learning and growing, to visualize their own career path. I have figured out how to be successful in my field. I want my people to have that too.

MOTIVATION
THE POWER OF INTENTION

I want to talk a little bit about your unconscious mind. When you say to yourself, "I'm going to expand this shop someday, or I want a second location one day," the mind accepts it literally. Thinking in the future keeps the mind in a constant state of "someday" (a.k.a. not right now). Instead say, "I am. I do...I book $1,000 a day. I own a forty-million-dollar-per-year hair care company. I am an author; I travel and speak; I am a dynamic speaker." Whatever your particular dreams and goals are, think of them in the present.

I saw my salon finished before I even had a location. I saw the product line I now produce ten years before it existed. I envisioned the income that's happening now as if it was real. I saw it happen before it happened.

To give an example from my personal life, one of the

things I always wanted to do was play lead guitar in a band like Eric Clapton or Stevie Ray Vaughn. I wanted to be the guy ripping through a solo with a crowd of screaming fans at my feet. When I figured out the power of intention and visualization, I started imagining my future concerts from the point of view of the stage. I would close my eyes and see those audience members going nuts. It took a little time away from my business to achieve that goal; however, it happened for my band. We built a solid following in the Ohio River Valley, and we ripped heads. It was awesome.

When you imagine someday, that kicks your unconscious into neutral. *Is someday tomorrow? After retirement?* It doesn't know. That's why I teach my new talent to picture the finished haircut they're working on before it's complete. I say, "What's it like finished? Close your eyes for a second; see it finished." When I'm coaching small business owners, I take the same approach. Ask yourself that question about your dream operation. "What does it look like when it's finished?"

Once you do that sort of visualization, the next steps reveal themselves.

1. Use active "I am" statements when you daydream.
2. When you visualize, use your unconscious as a power source. Tell it what you'll see when you have achieved the goal, and it will start working on the problem.
3. I've said it before. Dream big.

LEAD WITH INTENTION

During my first seven years of salon ownership, my leadership lacked energy. There wasn't any strength behind my decisions. When I finally made the decision to really be *in* business, that statement became a magnet. Deciding that work would happen my way or no way, that decision had resonance. Because there was such strong energy in that way of being, people started finding me. That power became a magnet for other powerful people.

Some people call this the law of attraction. I'm not picky about labels, but it's true that you reap what you sow. My strongest people, the ones who have been with me years and years, were attracted to the structure and leadership I created. There's an aura of energy that happens when a firm decision is made. Now that I'm aware of how that works, I can see it all around me.

People who have strong character and are motivated won't last five minutes arounds folks that don't. That's why I tore through nine salons in nine years. **The weak cannot lead the strong.** It's oil and water. As a business owner, if you want a world-class staff, you must provide them with an environment that allows them to thrive. Then you have to challenge them.

I've mentioned a few times the one employee who stuck with me through the major walkout. Her name is Kelly. She is one of the stylists earning serious money these days; the younger hairdressers even have a name for her level of achievement. They say, "I want to earn Kelly Money!"

Some years back, we were doing a workshop at a large, successful beauty school owned by a friend of mine in Omaha, Nebraska. He conducts a lot of advanced training for the hairdressing community, and he had invited me in as the feature guest artist for an audience of eighty to 100 members.

Kelly had joined me for the workshop; at that point, she had maybe three or four years in as a stylist. She was in her mid-20s then and just starting to get busy behind the chair. In the audience, there were a lot of twenty-five-plus years hair vets staring back at us. It had the potential to be very intimidating.

I said to Kelly, "Now, here's what I want you to do. Take our model, this young lady here, go out there on the stage, and do this haircut." I handed her a picture of a haircut we had been doing recently. She looked at me like I was out of my mind.

"No way. There's no way I'm going out there."

I said, "Kelly, take this model, go out there on the stage, and do this haircut."

"I'm not doing it. I came here to support you. I'm not going out there and doing that haircut; I'm not doing it; I'm not doing it. You want that haircut so bad, you freakin' go do it! You're not making me do it!"

She started tearing up and I said, "Kelly, take this girl, go out there on the stage, and do that haircut." And she did. She's never looked back. Kelly hated me at that moment, but she's one of the most highly paid stylists in the country, working four days a week. She's the queen bee now.

My point? I could have easily done that demo, but that wouldn't have pushed Kelly to the next level of her career. You don't gain skills by standing on the sidelines watching. A good leader moves you to places you haven't been, places that you probably wouldn't go on your own. You might fantasize about it, thinking, "Maybe I will try that sometime ..."—but a quality leader will push you to make it happen.

I have a philosophy with my companies now. I say to my employees, "Fail? That's not happening on my watch. If you want to go down the street and fail somewhere else, that's your business, but you ain't doing it here."

That philosophy, of teaching my team members to fly, has taken on a life of its own. Some of my employees have gotten so good at teaching others, and being leaders themselves, that I couldn't be prouder of them.

I think there are business owners who come to the point where their second in command knows just as much as them, and they find it threatening. It's almost like they're in competition with their people. Let me urge you to avoid that pitfall. **You want your employees to outperform you.** You want them to be smarter than you.

Four years ago, I actually stopped taking appointments. I have other revenue streams that are taking more time now. It's where I want to focus my energy, and it's allowing me to continue to grow. My salon is growing faster than it ever has, because I have many colonels and majors who keep salon operations tight in my absence. They don't need me there every day, and I love it. That means I'm free to build a distribution business or write a book. Or ride my motorcycle!

To ensure that these highly valuable leaders stay with me, I offer equity. For example, Lindsay has been with me for a decade. She's extremely smart, and I'm very, very proud of her. She's got wherewithal and determination and frankly, she deserves to be a partner. She works as hard as I do on the business. I made the equity offer for two reasons.

With equity, Lindsay has even more motivation to help build this thing (that is now part hers). Her efforts add value; therefore, the business is worth more now; therefore, she should benefit too.

From a business standpoint, it was the smart thing to do.

The bottom line is, would you rather have a percentage of an operation worth ten million dollars or 100% of an operation worth zero?

CHAPTER 8

HOW TO WIN

PICTURE ME IN 1995. I'M SITTING IN THE EMPLOYEE BREAK ROOM AT THE SALON, EATING LUNCH AND THUMBING THROUGH AN INDUSTRY JOURNAL.

I see a notice about the biggest awards in beauty, the North American Hairstyling Awards (NAHA). The winners are there on the page, holding their trophies, grinning enormously. These are the Oscars of hairstyling. Everyone in the industry attends.

Now, before I tell you how I reacted, pause and consider what you would do in that situation. When confronted with evidence of someone else's success do you: Feel happy for them? Jealous of them? Angry that you aren't up there too? Inspired to be like them?

The exercise is helpful, because it shows you what your unconscious mind thinks about success. Once you have that information, you can start using your unconscious to your advantage.

When I looked at that page, I thought, "I can do that!" and then immediately after, "I'm coming to get you." Within seconds, I had a new goal. Still holding my sandwich, I visualized myself in that audience of beauty and fashion editors and salon industry executives. The announcers called my name, "The winner is Bennie Pollard!"

In my fantasy, I went up to the stage and looked out over the hundreds of faces, took a deep breath, and started to speak confidently. I was rehearsing my acceptance speech before I even entered the competition.

MOTIVATION
THREE QUESTIONS

As I said in the last chapter, thinking about your future wins as if they have already happened spurs your unconscious into action mode.

To extend the lesson of visualizing your wins before they happen, let me show you another way our thoughts determine our success. I've witnessed this scenario play out many times. Let's say there are two stylists (or two bakers or two dentists…it doesn't matter what industry). They are the same age, same talent level, and start the same year. One person's earnings rocket to the stratosphere; the other has to take a second job or eventually leaves the industry altogether. Despite the exact same opportunities, what caused that difference in success?

As I see it, the only variable that is truly different is their thoughts. How do they feel about themselves? What do they say when confronted with an opportunity?

Is it: "I can't do it?"

Or: "I make shit happen."

These particular thoughts are important to pay attention to within your own mind, because they show how you feel about yourself. Do you think you are worthy of success? Or does a part of you refuse to allow it? Further complicating matters, sometimes we blame others when we are afraid of not achieving. It sounds something like, "I can't because (someone else) needs my time," or "That other person always gets the new clients. The front desk hates me."

All of us have this inner dialog. Often there's one side arguing against the other, kind of like the angels and devils you see perched on cartoon characters' shoulders. These characters are your unconscious beliefs. Often, without us even realizing it has happened, those beliefs will talk us out of greatness before we've even noticed they're there. They say things like, "I can't. There's no way to (fill in the blank): grow in this market, hire more staff, or get my employees to do that). It's just not possible."

When you catch your beliefs preaching negativity, like a devil on your shoulder, stop and ask these three questions:

1. Where did that belief come from?
2. Is it true?
3. Will it help me or hurt me?

This approach requires some honesty with yourself. Are you sure you can't stretch and add more clients to your day? Does believing that you can't help you—or does it hurt you?

The first thing that happens when people start challenging their deeply-ingrained negative thoughts is an internal fight. Be prepared for your negative beliefs to talk even louder about how you can't achieve. Over time, you can retrain that devil to say positive things.

"I can work faster. I book $1,000 a day. I am worthy of success."

1. Pay attention to your inner conversations. Realizing that they're there is the first step to changing them.
2. If your beliefs discourage you from risk, ask the three questions.
3. Re-write the negative statements into positive ones.

As soon as I saw that NAHA-winning photo, I started thinking which category I would enter and pulling together models to do a photo shoot. All the while, I replayed my winning visualization over and over. Lo and behold, I was nominated the first year I entered!

I took my mom with me to the event, certain I would be making a speech in front of her and the rest of the room. There was a nice dinner. We had a wonderful night together. Then, the awards ceremony began; they called all the winner's names—but not mine. I didn't win. Don't get me wrong, just being nominated was absolutely an honor. I was proud to be operating at this new echelon, but I wanted to win—*dammit*. I was indignant that they didn't pick me. I decided that, of course, I would do it again.

The next year, I entered even more categories and got nominated for two awards. And I didn't win again! I thought, for sure, there were politics involved. The NAHA judging process goes through two blind rounds: industry people and then editorial staff from the big fashion magazines like *Glamour, Vogue,* and *Elle*. "The fix is in," I remember saying, as bitterness momentarily crept in. I was so pissed that I just about decided never to enter again.

But I had to keep going. Something inside me was determined to show those people, and the rest of my industry, that I was just as good as they were. I kept shooting photos and entering,

shooting and entering. I wasn't even nominated in '98 and '99. In 2000, I got another nomination. I remember giving an interview during the lead up week where I compared myself to Susan Lucci, the soap opera actress who was nominated nineteen times before finally winning an Emmy.

I didn't win that year either.

Then finally, in 2003, eight years after I first started trying, I won a NAHA award...in the hardest category: avant-garde. Avant-garde hair is all about the art and seeing just what fantasy you can bring to life. You might see hair like that on a Paris runway or a *Vogue* fashion layout. I found it very exciting, because I could push the envelope. I designed and created all the wardrobe, I made all the hair pieces and wigs, and I always directed all the photography. I did everything except push the shutter closed on the camera. The man behind the camera and the guy who handled the exceptional lighting was my longtime friend Ed Brown. The third member of our dynamic trio was the very talented Lesa Miller, a celebrated make-up artist of the year and indispensable to my presentation. I could not have done it without those two.

After trying and failing for so long, the win felt sweet. It felt like getting a monkey off my back. My mom had been to every single award ceremony; she watched as I lost over and over. So, my acceptance speech was all about her and how she had worked so hard for her babies all those years. It was my way to say thank you to her.

I feel like there was a reason I had to wait so long to finally earn that first NAHA award. People told me later, "Oh, you were at the right place at the right time." Well, that doesn't mean jack shit if you're not the right person at the right place at the right time. Most lottery winners wind up broke. They weren't the right person to get that kind of windfall.

That was true with me too. I wasn't the right person to make money or win awards in my early career. I had to work on me for a while before I could start attracting any kind of income or accolades.

When NAHA nominated me the second time, in 2007 for the category Contemporary Classic, I no longer felt that anger about proving myself. I thought, if I won, it was a perfect time to use this experience to advance my business and my profession.

Like in 2003, I had a well-researched speech. This time, free from my angst about getting recognized, I saw an opportunity to make a serious impression on my industry. I wanted this speech to be more than just a hectic list of names sandwiched in between, "Ohmigod!" and "Ican'tbelievethis!"

I could believe it; I had been planning on it for nearly a decade.

I wanted this to be an inspirational moment that included everyone in the room. I started by saying, in essence, there's no such thing as self-made people, only self-starters. I thanked my wife, my mom, and my team. To finish my speech, I invited the audience to be a part of my celebration. I asked them to shout the phrase, "Without us!" at the end of my every sentence.

I said, "There's not a movie made in Hollywood—without us!"

"There's not a television show produced—without us!"

"There aren't any weddings—without us!"

"There aren't any proms—without us!"

"There aren't any Oscars—without us!"

"There isn't even a funeral—without us!"

After the award ceremony, I could feel from the reactions I got that the approach had worked. People did respond to the "without us" idea. They appreciated being lifted up with me.

Maybe you're asking why you should care about my wins. I'll give you two reasons.

Believing in yourself enough to visualize the end result increases your chances of it becoming reality. There is great power in focusing on your ideal outcomes.

When your wins come, recognize them for what they are—spring boards waiting to launch you even higher. Honors that garner attention are a huge opportunity to magnify your business growth. With my speech, I parlayed one win into exponential wins…and I did it in real time—not after I got home and had time to re-group. I knew going in, I'd have about four minutes on stage. I asked myself, *What kind of impact can I have on my industry in four minutes?*

Looking backwards, I can see my career evolved in three stages. Because of questionable upbringing, my early motivation to succeed was to prove wrong every single person who said I couldn't do it. My first fifteen years as a working professional was fueled by that fear. After that, I wanted to prove to myself that I really was the person I had been trying to become. After I gained some confidence and maturity, I wanted to open the door for others. In a lot of ways, that's why this book exists. I want many more people to buy into belief that what they do is important, and that they can—and should—stand up and go for it.

MOTIVATION
TENACITY

My first NAHA win wouldn't have happened had I not been so determined to show everyone I could do it. It made me go after a win that much harder.

I could have thrown in the towel. Losing sucks, it's embarrassing, and it was expensive. An average shoot (at that time) was costing me $8,000 for models, film, time, and supplies. I was mad as a hornet thinking, "You know what? I'm coming—and I'm gonna take all of you out." For me, losing was a motivator.

It felt like NAHA was saying, "You're never gonna be anything."

I responded with, "Oh, really."

It was personal, and I'll admit I had a chip on my shoulder. There was no way I was going to back down from that fight.

What do I mean by tenacity? It's having sheer determination, gumption, chutzpah, or moxie—whatever word we want to use. It's the willingness to fail repeatedly and continue to get up. It's the driving force behind just about all major advancements in the world.

Can you be successful in business without tenacity? I think yes…with a qualifier. As a business owner, you must have some stubbornness. You don't have to be as bull-headed as I am about it, but you've got to have some fight, because business is brutal. At any level, you must expect to get knocked down, especially if you have employees. Without tenacity, that's an ass whooping waiting to happen. When all you really want to do is throw in the towel, tenacity will get you back in the ring.

Where does tenacity come from? Your internal motivation will be individual to you. If you're not sure about your own drive, you can use the three questions from earlier in this chapter to figure out what your unconscious thinks about your success. I discovered, as I learned about unconscious motivators, that mine was a piss-and-vinegar reaction to hearing naysayers in my early years. My inner voice said, "I'll show you."

You may have something similar driving your efforts.

I'm not saying that's all bad. Having spent so long wanting to prove others wrong, my advice is to be sparing about accomplishments as revenge. You can get started with that fuel, but it's not a good long-term solution. As I grew, the chip on my shoulder finally fell off. Yours might too, and you can replace it with a desire to have some pride in your performance. Or maybe you'll find a way to lead others to their success. There's no sweeter satisfaction than helping others find their song.

1. Accept, in advance, that missteps will happen.
2. Know in your head you are already a champion, waiting to be discovered. Your time to be celebrated will come.
3. You don't have to be a jackass who won't let go of every idea. However, you *do* have to be willing to fight for your dreams, even when it's hard.

These days, I'm still getting mileage off my wins at NAHA. My business is known as the only place in the Ohio Valley that does hair at such an advanced level. That reputation keeps the salon packed and attracts killer talent. When I recruit from beauty schools, I'll show them videos of our photo shoots. The behind-the-scenes excitement of us doing glamourous and cutting-edge work always gets their attention. Then I say, "We're the only people within 100 miles who do anything like this. If you want a piece of that, and you think you've got what it takes, give me your resume." Like I did for Kelly, I'm showing new staff what a possible career path might look like and nudging them in that direction. I'm opening the door for others and hoping to inspire the next generation of badass hairdressers, who will lead the industry long after I'm gone.

NUTS & BOLTS
THE POWER OF INDUSTRY GROUPS

As you can tell, I'm a strong proponent of membership in industry groups. Name a job, there's an umbrella association for it that offers education, networking, and advocacy for that profession. By joining, you're declaring your commitment to your field, measuring yourself against the best of your profession, and staying up to date on developments. Plus, there are often contests and awards. Always enter them.

I feel like there's no better way to prove yourself than to compete against the best of your peers. It's basic PR; I get to keep my business's name in the upper echelon of the beauty world. I want the industry's best and brightest to know I'm at their level and to think of me when they need something, whether that's a business partner or a magazine feature subject.

1. Find the most powerful industry association in your profession.
2. Join it.
3. Attend the meetings and enter their competitions.

CHAPTER 9

WHAT I SHOULD HAVE KNOWN

I'VE HAD MANY HONORS AND WINS IN MY CAREER. SOME I WAS READY FOR. OTHERS, NOT SO MUCH.

That *Glamour Magazine* mention in 1996 took my precarious business structure and blew it over like the big bad wolf. Compare that brush with success to the boom in business I experienced after my NAHA wins. Talented stylists wanted to work for the guy with a name in the industry. Customers wanted to come to the rockin', hot salon. Volume was up, and this time I was ready to grow.

Why did one opportunity nearly ruin me and the other launch me higher? The short answer is: I had learned how to run a business. My staff and my processes were rock-solid, because I built repeatable processes I could control—processes that ensured high quality experiences every time.

Could I have done that from the beginning? In theory, yes; but in reality, no. I knew what I should be doing, but I was too scared at the time. I had to fail hard to see that half-assed leadership won't cut it. Once I made the decision to be *in* business and be the boss, I gained the courage to set standards and stick to them. Because I felt confident, my people felt confident in me. That positive energy drew more motivated people to me.

The moment you declare yourself is the moment good things start lining up for you. That doesn't mean you'll be cruising down easy street forever after. There are still challenges and struggles for me, but I'm not grappling with doubt. Free from that mental baggage, I have more clarity to make the right decisions.

⚡

MOTIVATION
DON'T BELIEVE EVERYTHING YOU THINK

In the last chapter, I wrote about the three questions I use and teach to examine my inner life. When a doubt pops up, I ask: Where did that belief come from? Is it true? Will it help me or hurt me?

I want to be clear, there's still a lot of work to do after the moment you realize you're holding onto a false belief. Just because you recognize it as false doesn't mean you can blow it away like a dandelion seed. There's a reason for that.

As kids, we're told, "No, stop, don't!" over and over and over. To be fair to our parents, most of those admonishments are the only thing keeping us alive in our young years. "No touching the hot stovetop!" and "Don't lick the toilet!" are solid words to live by. The problem comes when, as older kids and teenagers, the "No, stop, don't!" messages continue to vastly outweigh phrases like: "Go for it!" or "Yes, you can do that!" We carry all those warnings with us into adulthood and, unconsciously, start saying them to ourselves. The cautions have their place. "No, stop, don't" is the only appropriate response to driving after a night of drinking, for example.

Yet, we often talk ourselves out of risks that would be beneficial. Should you join that networking group? Can you increase your prices? Should you attend professional development training? If your first answer is always no, you need to ask why not. A common excuse for adults is, "I don't have time." I want to encourage you to probe that answer. Our first-ditch excuses are rarely the real reason we choose not to do something.

Where did that belief come from? Is it true? Will it help me or hurt me?

Digging under, "I don't have time," might reveal something closer to, "I'm afraid."

So often, we operate on auto-pilot, driven by cautions that should have expired long ago. The three questions make you aware of your thoughts and what they're doing to you. Realizing you are afraid of something doesn't change your fear; however, recognizing its presence gives you the opportunity to change it. Awareness is the only way we can make changes.

I'm not saying you should commit to every single invitation. Time and priority constraints are real. I am urging you to be conscious about your choices. Know the "why" underneath the "no."

1. Pay attention to your thoughts, especially if you are turning down an opportunity.
2. Give yourself permission to have uncomfortable feelings. Sit with them.
3. Change comes after awareness.

As I worked to change my inner self, I started seeing chances to extend that positivity into my corner of the world. That's what I hope for you too; it's the reason I wrote this book. I hope you'll reach a plane of stability and maturity that gives you the confidence to extend opportunities to others in your sphere of influence. As Gandhi famously said, "Be the change you wish to see in the world."

SPREADING POSITIVITY

One of the perks of being a hairdresser is the customer reaction when I take their cape off. The number one thing I hear is, "Ah, I feel so much better." I know that people on the outside of the beauty business sometimes consider the pursuit of perfect hair vain or unimportant. On the inside of the business, I can testify that a simple cut and color goes much deeper. "I feel so much better," is real. My clients aren't saying, "I look better than her." They're saying I *feel* better about *myself*. I've seen ladies tear up in the chair, "Oh my God, is that me?" That's how I know I'm really working on their self-esteem.

With the ability to impact people on such a personal level, I realized I could affect real change in the world, beyond my salon. In the early 2000s, I had been tinkering with the idea of launching a new revenue stream, a product line that could be sold in salons across the country. Based on my clients' in-person reactions, I knew this was another opportunity to boost self-esteem.

My brand launched in 2001. Called BennieFactor, it plays off the word benefactor. Each product is named after a positive affirmation, because I want people who use it to take a sense of power or confidence with them into their day. For example, the thickening agent is called b More; the moulding putty is b Daring; the styling spray is b Confident. I imagined a woman getting ready for the day, thinking about her to-do list. I wanted the last thing she saw before she left to be affirming. She gives one last spritz of b Confident spray and says to herself, "Now, go get it." That was the whole essence of the brand.

Some may say that higher profit for me is in conflict with altruism. I beg to differ. I could make money doing a lot of things,

flipping houses for one. My worldview says: **true wealth is created by service**. The more people you serve, obviously, the more money you make. As a stylist, I was impacting people's lives one at a time, behind the chair. As a salon owner, I was able to impact twenty, thirty, or forty people at any one given time. As a manufacturer and distributor, I'm able to impact tens of thousands. Here's the point: the better I do, the more people I'm able to lift up, and the more people I can help to feel good about their value and ability to contribute. I want to leave the world better than I found it. Like Steve Jobs said, "I'm trying to make a dent in the universe."

That's what I hope for you too.

NUTS & BOLTS
CONTRIBUTE

When you grow financially, you become more able to contribute to society as a whole. First, I can contribute more money to charities, similar to what Bill and Melinda Gates are doing. Non-profit organizations depend on their local business communities to survive. Look around for a cause you are passionate about and make a donation. One of my favorites is the ASPCA, because I love animals.

Second, I can contribute through my spending, which supports other local enterprises. For example, I buy a new car. The purchase supports a local dealership. It also helps their distributor, because now they need to restock. And it helps the manufacturer of the car, because they will now get another order, and so on down the supply chain. All those individuals are more able to provide for their families. That participation in the economy only happens when a person has some level of financial success.

1. Having money affords you the ability to play a part in the health of your community.
2. You can do that through donations to worthy organizations.
3. Shopping is another way to stimulate your local economy.

I want you to explore your quiet, inner dreams and decide that you can go for it too. Small business owners have a lot of opportunity to positively impact others in many different ways. That's one of the really good things about being a small business person; you can have a meaningful impact on your world, because the interactions are so personal. It's the personal touches that make a difference in people's lives, and all of us can do that.

For example, think about a magnetic spot in your town that customers flock to. Maybe it's a microbrewery, a coffee shop, a pancake house, or a barber shop...the product or service doesn't really matter. The bigger reason behind loyal patronage is the vibe. People can buy beer all over the place, they come hang out at that particular location because they *feel better* when they come. Situations like that don't arise accidentally. They happen because the owner created an intentionally uplifting experience. All services or products that people bond with are connected to a deeper, human emotion. Mine happens to be self-esteem. What's yours? Is it peacefulness? Joy? Health? What's the deeper reason people come back to you? When you have that answer, you know where to start building positivity into your brand.

We all have the power to spread positivity. You don't have to start a non-profit, humanitarian organization to affect change in your community. Often, it's simply the act of knowing who you are and offering that authenticity that is such a draw.

That's how it's been for me. Once I figured out how to be more positive in my own life, I started impacting others. Long before I had won awards or started a salon, I was extending excitement—simply because spreading smiles gave me a thrill. The first time I discovered that, I was speaking at a Boston hairdresser's convention in the 90s. Up on the stage, I did my thing: cool hair, little bit of my beliefs, positive thinking stuff—a little Zig Ziglar. One of my main themes was, "Get out there and be yourself, man. Play whatever music you want to play in the salon. You want to play Led Zeppelin, you play it. Create your vibe; do good hair; set your goal. You dream your dreams." After that speech, I didn't think anything else of it.

I came back the following year to speak again, and a woman came up to me. "Oh my God, you're here again! You were the best thing that ever happened to me." I was amazed that she remembered me. I didn't even know what I was doing yet. Still, something I said helped her. That's when it first occurred to me that I could have a larger impact on others. And the point is, you can too.

So that you are not surprised by it, I want to add a word of caution about reaching beyond the status quo. Exploring your dreams comes at a cost. When you start transforming your ambitions into reality, expect some push-back. Sadly, that negativity often comes from those who are close to you. Okay, it *always* comes from those who are close to you. Here's why. People are scared of climbers. When they say, "You can't do that," what they mean is, "I don't think I can do that, so you shouldn't either." If you succeed, you're going expose their inertia. That will happen—go for it anyway. A friend who secretly hopes you'll fail isn't a friend.

MOTIVATION
LIFE IS A MARATHON

When I was younger, I was a busy guy—killing it on every front I could get access to. Yet, when I achieved the goals I set for myself, the reward felt anticlimactic and empty. I'd go, "Wait. This is it?" Then, off I'd go to the next thing—then the next thing. Finally, I realized I was waiting to be happy until I got there instead of savoring the awesome moments as they occurred. The problem with that approach is, there is no "there." We never "arrive." Once a goal is hit, motivated folks like us automatically up the ante. Sometimes we even say, "If somebody like me can get this prize, it's probably not even that good." You need to know that part of success is raising the bar on yourself. It's okay to never arrive. The joy in life comes through experiencing your process and growth. Savor the cool moments as they happen.

1. Relax.
2. Pace yourself.
3. Life is a marathon.

CHAPTER 10

REQUIRED SKILLS

AS A YOUNG MAN, BACK WHEN I QUIT ALL THOSE SALONS, I WAS LOOKING FOR A LEADER TO FOLLOW.

I wanted to find someone like my first boss at the country club, Mr. Griff; someone who gave orders and expected them to be followed, someone who was pursuing a vision. I looked high and low across two states and, after being disappointed repeatedly, I ultimately had to become the leader I needed. Through that, I figured out what a boss should be. There are the usual attributes: visionary, profit-driven, decisive, and confident...but let me add one that's not on all the lists. **A bottom-line goal of a solid leader should be to create more leaders.**

I know I have said that your employees must follow orders. That's true with a caveat. I encourage my people to have ideas and share them *once they have proven they know the basics.* It's like anything creative; you've got to learn the rules before you can break them.

At my salon, the training program and stellar senior stylists give new staff examples to follow and a spark to envision success. All those savvy professionals got me thinking. *Why should they all be working at a salon with my name on it?* I recently rebranded the business as Nova Salon, so that it's no longer tied to me personally. My staff doesn't need me there every day, and I love that. The new name will also make future multiple locations stronger since potential customers won't have to ask, "Who's this Bennie guy?"

I am so grateful to be surrounded by rock star leaders who have helped me grow my business, who have become more successful, and who made me more successful as a result. My team is full of leaders, and that's on purpose.

To me, proof of trailblazer status is a willingness to pass the torch to others. If you're going be an employer, then you have a responsibility to ensure the long-term success and personal growth of everyone in your employ. If you're not willing to do that, then get the hell out of our way. You are unworthy of being an employer.

That may be a controversial statement; however, I mean it, because I learned the lesson the hard way. Being someone's boss is serious business. You're messing with people's lives; you've got to take the responsibility seriously. When bosses suck, their employees suffer through no fault of their own. I have a theory that the largest scale example of poor leadership happened when the economy crashed in 2008. In the wreckage of that catastrophe, a whole chunk of forty-five to fifty-year olds were whacked. They had invested ten, twenty, or even thirty years at their companies; they should have been experts in their fields. Why were they the victims?

The prevailing wisdom said those people got laid off because they cost too much, and younger kids were hungry to perform and cheaper to employ. That may be part of it; I see it differently. I believe they lost their jobs because they weren't being held to any kind of responsible standard of performance (or simply corporate politics). Employees should be thought of as company assets. Handled correctly over decades of working, it should be unthinkable to let them go.

STARTING MY CONSULTING GROUP

As my salon evolved, I kept percolating on my vision of making a dent in the universe. *How could I make a difference in my corner of the world?* My staff proved the concept that my training program inspired innovators and leaders. As I looked around the country, there still weren't many salons running with vision and intention. Most salons aren't profitable; if the owner gets sick or steps away for any length of time, the business tanks. I realized others in my industry could use the same lessons I taught my employees. I wanted to start a product distribution and a consulting company to do just that.

At the same time, I realized I liked working directly with salons better than distributors. I had tried contracting with many distributors around the country to expand BennieFactor's reach. These sellers had my brands, but they had all the Godzillas of the product world too: like Paul Mitchell, Matrix, and Aveda. The sales people just weren't motivated to push my product when they had other, more familiar, brands that were easier to sell. In fact, I believe the bigger brands put pressure on the distributors *not* to sell little upstarts, like my brand, to preserve their profits. One distributor actually contracted to sell my line, and then buried it, hoping it would die. I knew if I could go talk to owners, I could sell BennieFactor, but some distributors wouldn't let me anywhere near salons. They were afraid a startup would cut into big brands' business. It seemed to me they were being held hostage.

With all that swirling in my head, I made a decision.

I would take back all the distribution of my product, *and* I would bring in the right partners. I met a sales consultant, and we became pals. His name is Jeff Petro and he was (and still is) the finest salon sales consultant I've seen in my entire career.

He wouldn't simply take the product order from the salons. He would sit down with business owners and teach them better ways to build their businesses...like a true consultant does.

When we first met, Jeff and I were competitors. That was in Indianapolis in 2003. After eighteen months of trying and failing, I had finally convinced the biggest, award-winning salon in the city to stock BennieFactor. The guy in charge of all the other product in that salon wondered, "Who in the heck just took a bite out of my sales?"

That was Jeff.

We met via a phone call, where we both huffed and puffed at each other for a while.

"How come you don't have distribution, Bennie?"

"I don't believe in distribution, Jeff."

"Really? You're going to go out there all by your lonesome?"

It was the posturing of a couple of alpha males, sizing one another up. Long story short, we became friends, and I realized Jeff is a badass ninja superstar, and I'd be foolish to waste the opportunity of meeting him.

In 2013, I invited Jeff to become a partner in Cool Beauty Consulting as sales director. Jeff and another of my home-grown superstars, Paula, became equity partners in the firm, and we were off to the races. Since its inception in 2013, Cool Beauty Consulting has grown every year.

At this point, let me share a few words with you about choosing a partner. First, be sure you really need one. So often, I find businesses struggling with leadership that boils down to a power struggle between the majority partners. When I ask the founder why they even invited the second person in, they say, "I was afraid I wouldn't be able to go it alone." Fear of personal failure isn't a reason to get a partner. Scaling a business up and requiring more manpower or a different set of complementary skills—that's a reason to include a new owner in the business. That's what Jeff and Paula are to me. All of our skills are very compatible. I'm macro; Jeff is micro; and Paula bridges the gap between us.

When you're ready to add another leader, you still need to adhere to three guidelines.

One, you must get along with each other.

Two, the new person should have a different skill set that supplements yours. No business can survive with two CEOs wrestling for the same territory.

Three, make clear guidelines on who does what.

Even if you're not ready to scale your business, there are important lessons to be learned here. For instance, get the right people around you. Success will happen based on who you're around as much as anything else. Identify a person who complements you, and don't fear their ability to compete with your achievements. As the saying goes, if you're the smartest person in room, you're in the wrong room. Keep an open mind—a student mind—as you discover brilliance.

Lastly, be persistent! You never know where your efforts will lead. When I went after the big-shot Indianapolis salon, I didn't know it would lead to my partnership with Jeff. If I had given up after a year of trying, who knows if I would have come up with the idea for Cool Beauty Consulting.

NUTS & BOLTS
DISTRIBUTORS HAVE WISDOM

What I'm about to tell you has relevance to all small businesses, whether yours is a salon, a restaurant, a veterinary practice, or a fence-building company. Most businesses think about price only when they should be asking, "What can my business become?" Price might be a part of the conversation, but I'd rather pay someone two cents more per unit and get their knowledge in the bargain.

Savvy distributors have a wealth of industry knowledge that could work to your benefit. They've spent time in all your competitors' businesses, good and bad. They have seen what worked and what fell flat. Ask them for advice. Maybe they have suggestions for scripting customer interactions or a more profitable way to build a schedule. Some companies even have educators who can come in and work with your team.

This advice isn't in the mainstream, however, I believe it should be. Distributors have untapped resources. Take thirty minutes away from "making the donuts" and have a conversation with them. See what they can give you beyond filling an order. If they're not moving your game forward, then you need to be looking around for a new supplier.

1. Distributors can give you more than supplies.
2. Always be learning.
3. Align yourself with people who will help you build your dream business.

With my new distribution company, I set about offering my products and several others I believe in, as well as all the proven training elements my in-house staff have access to. Cool Beauty Consulting now offers clinics across the Midwest, the Ohio Valley, and beyond.

What are we teaching? Many of the concepts that are in this book. Branding, marketing, speaking, networking, apprenticeship programs, bookkeeping, and goal setting are among them. I'm essentially sneaking in the business acumen I know they need, while providing the product they want.

Why are we teaching those concepts?

As I built the business model for Cool Beauty, I realized the seminars I had been offering as a platform artist were cool. The audiences loved them for the sexy hair, the power of positive thinking, and the cutting techniques. However, what the beauty professionals really needed wasn't flash and zing. They needed business expertise. If you're unable to understand a P&L, it won't matter if you're God's gift to hairdressing. I'm trying to build complete people as well as kick-ass stylists. Maybe these folks will go on to run their own salon, or maybe they'll switch professions and open a bar. Either way, the skills they get from me will transfer.

For you, I've broken down some of the concepts we teach through Cool Beauty. They transfer easily to other industries, and I believe they should be incorporated into all small business models.

GOAL SETTING

At Nova Salon, we require all staff to physically handwrite out their stats at the end of each day. We even created a workbook for this purpose. I think it's important to spend time with pen and paper, because the more senses a person engages, the deeper their understanding of the information. Slowing down and getting personal with your data helps you consider it more deeply.

Even though my computer systems and data systems have everything I need, I still require the stylists to sit still with their workbook every day. They record the total number of clients, clients requested, new clients, client services, retail products sold, and how many people rescheduled that day.

I'm encouraging them to pay attention, because what you measure grows. Keep score, do more. Part of the reason our highest earner, Kelly, has been with us so long is because she was able to watch that money grow over time. That accomplishment is empowering in a way that no pep talk will ever be. Now, every January, she looks back at the previous January and plans out an entire year of earning.

I would encourage you to do the same thing. Keep a daily written record of your earnings and your projected goal. Break down the sales or hours worked that get you to that goal. As you track, you'll inevitably start thinking of ways to get faster or more efficient with your invested time. Which leads to the next tip, which I call power booking.

POWER BOOKING

Power booking is my term for the most efficient workflow available to a service business. It's similar to how a doctor and nurse work together. The nurse sees you first, then communicates with the doctor. Then, the doctor does his or her thing. It works the same way on a sales floor. The first person who helps you on the Harley Davidson dealership floor is probably not the same person you'll be working with on financing and contracts. When your staff can separate tasks, your overall business can serve more people in a day, which obviously means more money in the door.

In the salon, our power-booking procedures start a client with the front desk staff. If they're new to the salon, the styling apprentice gives the client a tour of the business to help them understand the level of service we offer and help them feel comfortable. They offer the client a beverage, then escort the client to the senior stylist's chair for the image profile conversation. After that, the apprentice shows the client to the shampoo room, which we call the cleansing center. There, the lights are dimmed and talking is kept to a minimum, so clients can relax and enjoy the scalp massage and shampoo experience. In this way, stylist time is reserved for design tasks only and apprentices get experience caring for clients. When color is a part of the appointment, the apprentice steps in for the color application and manages the color-setting time. Bluntly put, senior designers shouldn't be doing apprentice work, because their time is more valuable than that.

This is the apprenticeship model I learned from Immy all those years ago, but now it's on steroids. I've added far more structured timing and procedures to the framework, because it promotes multiple goals simultaneously: it makes the salon more profitable, it makes the stylists themselves more profitable, and stylists get to teach the apprentices—teaching and training others actually helps the stylists grow too. You teach, you get better. The apprentices see what a career path might look like, based on the experiences of the veteran staff members.

Plus—and this is key—when each customer engages with multiple staff members during a visit, they get used to being in different people's chairs. This practice makes them customers of the *salon* rather than the individual stylist. So, when one person is too busy, she or he can pass on clients to other staff members. For example, if the client can't get the time they want, or prices have increased beyond their budget, they already feel comfortable with other staff members. The switch to a different stylist becomes much easier. Most importantly, they stay with the salon. That's insurance for your team members and you.

I realized how crucial that method of booking was when I was injured in a traffic accident. Home with two cracked wrists, I was out for five weeks. At the time, I was the highest earner in the salon, so I saw a drastic hit in cash flow. What would happen to your business if you couldn't be there for two months? Would the doors still be open when you got back? Build your staff workflow so it works without you there, and so other key employees have as much of a shot to be big earners as you do.

SCRIPTING

When clients call Nova Salon, they hear, "Thank you for choosing Nova Salon, where we love every hair on your head. My name's Bennie. How may I assist you?" When a tour is given, there's a script for that, and we require staff to rehearse the speech. We have scripts for stylists as well. An image profile always starts exactly the same way.

"What was the best salon experience you ever had?"

Then, "What was your favorite haircut you ever had?"

There's a method and a reason for all of these practices. I have found, over time, that this is the best way to welcome my customers. To put it in music terms, these are the hits the fans want to hear. I want my fans (clients) to know from the first contact that our salon is different from any other they've visited. We're special—a place they will feel comfortable and drawn to. The next time they come, it will be exactly the same. There's comfort in consistency.

That doesn't mean clients should feel like factory parts running down an assembly line. We make sure all our team members understand their role. The scripts are written to provide a responsive, high-care setting for clients.

All this structure might sound off-putting to some. In the early days, I was a live-and-let-live kind of boss. That attitude ran my business right into the ground. From that, I learned leadership requires structure. That means staff must buy into my philosophy to work for me. I will not sacrifice the quality of customer experiences. Period. Sometimes my competitors try to discourage new beauty school graduates from coming to me by calling my staff Bennibots. As in, "You gonna go be a Bennibot? You don't want that."

Experienced staff don't mind structure; in fact, they like it. Strong and motivated people love organized systems like this. I take everything off their plate that gets in the way of creativity—no answering the phone, no greeting customers, and no scheduling appointments—only hair design. The scripts and predictability allow their creativity to soar; they're a benefit of employment. In fact, I discovered the more I systemized operations, the stronger the character of the individuals who wanted to work with me. When I decided to be the "hard ass", and make people dig in and do things the right way, the business exploded.

By the way, those front desk people? They're not high school kids. Businesses often try to save money by hiring someone cheap to man the phones and greet customers. That's nuts. That person is the first and last touch of your customers' experience. It's crucial they be professional at all times, which requires an adult. And to come back to my perpetual growth model, I'm grooming those front desk people to run their own stores one day.

CAREER PATH

With all new hires, we onboard them early to our vision for them. "This is what your year one will look like; year two you'll be here; year three here, and so on." Again, I'm building complete people. I'm inspiring them to dream beyond next week, which is actually rare in my industry. For better or worse, many folks who cut hair come from pretty humble beginnings. I can't tell you how many times I have heard someone say, "Well, Dad was over at the mine making $50,000 a year. That's good money."

No, it's not! No one told them they could earn over $100,000 per year, so it never occurred to them they could be more successful. So, I'm telling them. More importantly, I'm showing them *how* to earn $100,000 or more. I feel a responsibility to encourage those who are coming after me.

LIVING LAB

All those training aspects are built into the educational programs Cool Beauty Consulting offers customers. In addition, we allow them to come observe the methods in action at Nova Salon. We call it the Living Lab. Jeff Petro and I came up with the concept when we heard one too many participants say something like, "Oh, sure. Your people answer the phone that way, but mine never would." So, I started inviting them into my house, so to speak.

There's a cultural belief that seeing is believing. I actually feel the opposite is true (believe it, then you'll see it), but to help with the learning curve, I have found that showing versus telling is a stronger way to teach. A salon owner, and perhaps their manager or key stylist, attend a class session and then observe out on the floor, so they can watch this stuff happen. It's not in theory; this is the real thing. I know it works because I hear so many, "Oh, that's how you do it ..." comments.

For readers who aren't Cool Beauty Consulting clients, or don't work in the salon industry, I would encourage you to find your own living lab. Benchmark the best in your industry and ask if you can observe their operations. You don't have to recreate the wheel; why spend your time and energy inventing a new system when there's a model you could use as a template? Go find the best and learn from them.

MOTIVATION
KNOWLEDGE ISN'T POWER

Many of these ideas I'm sharing with you are elements of success I have known about for far longer than I've been using them. From way back, I studied mentors and business gurus. It took me much longer to implement practices I knew would work because of fear—or maybe maturity. In my 20's, I wasn't far enough along to embrace scripting as a management tool. I knew about it; I just didn't do it.

At the end of the day, it's not a lack of knowledge. Rather, it's people's fear of implementation that kills them; the knowledge is available. That's why I say that knowledge isn't power. Knowledge doesn't mean shit. Implementation and action are everything.

I remember the moment when I said to myself, "I don't care if I have to cut hair by myself, I know how I'm gonna do it. I know exactly what to do." It was after the walkout. I had to drive a business into the ground before getting the guts to lead the way I knew I should. The minute I made that decision, the right people started showing up.

1. You already know what you need to do to improve your business.
2. What are you waiting for?
3. Action is power.

CHAPTER 11

LEAVING YOUR MARK: BRANDING

WHEN THE WORD BRANDING COMES UP IN BUSINESS CIRCLES, IT USUALLY REFERS TO THE PHYSICAL ELEMENTS OF A BRAND LIKE LOGO, WEBSITE, AND CORPORATE COLOR PALETTE.

However, there's a whole lot more to it than that.

When I teach branding to my Cool Beauty Consulting clients, I include the following branding elements:

1. In-Person
2. Corporate and Physical
3. Emotional
4. Relationship
5. Systems

I believe you need all of these branding components running efficiently to truly distinguish your business from the herd. You might wonder if that's really necessary.

I'll tell you why it's absolutely necessary.

Let's say, for example, that in most cities, for every 100-mile radius there are about 500 salons—maybe less, maybe more. With an average of six stylists per salon, that's 3,000 hairdressers my potential clients have to choose from. In order to draw the type of client I want (the ones who are willing to pay top dollar and keep coming back), I need to be the very best. I need to be intentional with every choice I make and every interaction I have. Your sector may not be quite so saturated; however, no matter your business or industry, I guarantee you have competition. The questions to ask yourself:

"When customers could go anywhere, why should they choose me?"

"When I do get a shot with them, will they remember me the way I want to be remembered?"

NUTS & BOLTS
ON PURPOSE

If I could go back and visit yourself during your senior year of high school, what would your classmates say your brand was? How would they describe you? Smart aleck? Party animal? Serious athlete? Straight-A student? Actually, any answer you can come up with now is a total guess. Further, the same may still be true of you now, unless you're being deliberate about your brand.

If you're casual about how your business is perceived in the community, if you don't target and track, you're still guessing about how your customers see you. That's what I mean about being intentional with your brand. Most people run their lives on auto-pilot 99% of the time. However, when you're cognizant of your particular audience, you can be certain of how they perceive you.

1. Your brand is what you are putting out into the universe.
2. Most people don't pay much attention to their interactions, and thus their brand is haphazard.
3. By deliberately planning your behavior and messages, your brand becomes intentional.

9 ELEMENTS OF IN-PERSON BRANDING

In-person branding is all about emotional connections. These elements help your customers come to see you as a trusted resource. At first blush, these concepts probably seem like the kind of no-brainer stuff kids should be learning from parents or teachers. Yet, often, adults are missing those skills—or they've forgotten them. That's why I take the time and effort to break down these nine elements of in-person branding. If you're going to have employees, this is the first thing you should teach them.

1. EYE CONTACT

Finish this sentence: "I couldn't trust him...he wouldn't look me _____."

If you thought the blank should read "look me in the eye", you are in the majority. Most people believe eye contact is a sign of honesty. It isn't. I'm sure you have experienced someone looking you right in the eyeball and then lying through their teeth. The truism that eye contact equals honesty is completely false. I include this dichotomy here to illustrate the point that we all hold beliefs that aren't true. It's important to question your assumptions. That being said, most people believe it, so we need to adhere to the social practice of eye contact.

Experts say we have from seven to seventeen seconds of interacting with strangers before they form an opinion of us. What opinion do you leave people with if you won't even meet their gaze? The eyes are the window to the soul.

2. SMILE:

Smiles are contagious, and that's a good thing. I don't care if you only have one tooth—get it out there! My grandmother was ninety years old when she passed. Didn't have a tooth in her head. When she smiled, the whole room lit up. A smile shows others your **soul**.

Remember the emotional brand you want to build with your customers; you should be pleasant, professional, and interested. It doesn't matter if you are having a good day or not, you must SMILE.

3. HANDSHAKE

The classic business handshake is the most recognized greeting in the world. It says, I'm a person who respects you. It's also your chance to share a bit of your energy. When you want to do business with someone, you need to transfer confidence.

There's a caveat, however. A dead fish handshake will do more harm than good. A solid handshake, whether you are male or female, goes like this: web to web with the other person (the web is the tissue between your thumb and forefinger), with a quality, firm grip. Shake everyone's hand every visit.

Preserve the "intimacy zone" of eighteen inches between you. Some people say, "Well Bennie, I'm a hugger!" I say, "Great, I'm a hugger too, but you need permission before you get that close."

4. WARDROBE

When I started doing hair, it was the early 80s. MTV was new to the scene, and I emulated the craziest styles I saw. I looked like a cartoon character. I discovered that the way I was dressed did not reflect my intentions of becoming a smokin' stylist with an exclusive clientele. The ladies who could afford to pay what I wanted to charge didn't trust me with their look. They were wearing beautiful

Chanel, and I had on acid-washed, ripped denim and parachute pants—we need not go any further. I like to paraphrase one of Coco Chanel's famous quotes this way, "Fashion is fleeting; style is forever." I saw a different response from my target audience after I started dressing according to my business goals.

Carrying the wardrobe concept to my employees, their dress must also convey trust and consistency with the salon's brand. At my salon, all black is the dress code. If we really analyze the most successful companies out there, they require dress codes or uniforms. They are intentional in their packaging.

5. SCENT

The first thing most people do when they pick up a new bottle of hair product is open it and smell it. Scent is deeply emotional; one whiff of someone wearing your grandma's perfume can take you right back to her. Those are examples of pleasant smells and associations. The opposite is also true. Every stylist has at least one customer whose breath is so noxious, they can hardly bear to stand next to them. Be aware of your breath, your perfume, and your body odor. Take steps to ensure your customers leave your presence with only positive feelings about you.

6. POSTURE

How you carry yourself broadcasts your deepest emotions. Remember the story from Chapter 4 about the group of girls I saw one day? When the tallest of the bunch hunched over so much, it told me how uncomfortable she felt with her height. I didn't exchange a single word with her and yet, I knew her whole story. When you walk into your business, stand up straight. Your employees and your customers are waiting for you to set the tone. Posture displays your level of confidence.

7. DIALOGUE AND DELIVERY

In the digital age, we're inundated with a barrage of non-stop communication. All that noise leaves the door open for you to differentiate yourself. When talking to clients, leave space. Pause. Use inflection to stress important words.

How you say things is more important than what you say. For example, in my salon, it's important to have my customers schedule their follow-up appointments way in advance. Because they can't get in last minute, clients really do need to pre-schedule future visits. So, I say it this way.

> "Lisa, here's what I want you to do. [Pause] I want you to schedule your next *two* appointments today." [Hold up two fingers and stress the word "two" by raising your voice slightly.]

Like a musical score, my communication has rhythm and beat.

Think about the messages your customers must hear in order to get the best service, and then practice saying them with inflection and cadence. When possible, use visual communication as well. For instance, hold up the number of fingers and point to the sign. That way you're involving two senses and increasing retention of the message.

Well-timed pauses are the best way to get someone's attention. When we think about the words we are using, we'll be extremely effective in communicating our business values. Rather than rushing through a sentence, let it breathe. Let your customer's hearing catch up to what you are saying. For example, say, "When you purchase a full set of tires, [pause] you get lifetime alignments." As opposed to, "Hey,yougetlifetimealignmentswiththat."

8. PUNCTUALITY

How many of you readers have a friend, that no matter what you are doing, is *always* late? How many of you readers *are* that friend who's always late? Remember, time is non-refundable. Taking someone's time is theft. It's disrespectful. Early is on time.

9. ATTITUDE

My favorite speaker, Zig Zigler, famously said, "Your attitude always determines your altitude." Without a positive attitude, none of these other elements will make a bit of difference in your business. Be professional and friendly, no matter what you are feeling.

The next step for any fledgling company will be their physical attributes: what they look like to the public from a tangible standpoint.

CORPORATE BRANDING

Corporate branding is a large umbrella that encompasses your tangible elements. For instance, your printed materials like business cards, menus, and envelopes must be consistent—and mind blowing. These materials are very, very important, though some companies skimp here. A baker might choose to spend more for his oven than his public persona. That doesn't make any sense, because the behind-the-scenes gear won't get him new customers to bake for.

When I give someone a business card, if I don't get a positive comment on it, I need to re-do them right away. I want my card to be so freaking cool, they want to keep it whether we ever do business together or not. Shopping bags are the same. When your customers walk away with a purchase, they should think the bag is so cool, they want to hold onto it. Do you have a few high-end bags in a closet somewhere? That's tangible branding. Your attachment to the material (and thus, the brand) continues after you've finished up the product you bought.

If you really want to stand out from those other 3,000 hair-dressers—or those other 3,000 bakers—or those other 3,000 veterinarians—people have to want to keep your stuff. That's why I mentioned before: pay for graphic design and marketing expertise. Those services aren't do-it-yourself jobs any more than fixing your own transmission or coloring your own hair are.

In this same category of corporate branding comes your physical space. Things like chipped paint, stained ceiling tiles, and warped flooring all communicate a negative message. And here's where I want mention cleanliness. Start with your restrooms. No one wants to visit the proverbial gas station restroom. Don't be that kind of business.

EMOTIONAL BRANDING

The way the customer feels when they leave your store **is the brand**. Your business cards can be sexy as hell, and your in-person skills can be on point, but none of that matters if people feel a negative emotion when they walk through the door. The way that customer feels upon entering your space is almost as important as when they leave. Therefore, you must keep your floor mats straight, for crying out loud. If someone enters your front door and trips—in public—they immediately go into embarrassment mode. I call that red rush. They'll miss whatever it is you're bringing to the table, because they're still burning over falling on the rug. Even worse, that person will feel that emotion every time they come back. If they come back. So will the folks who witnessed it. Public embarrassment is that strong. Make the entryway safe.

Especially in my industry, customers are there for the feel-good experience. They say things like, "Ah, I feel better now." Clients are paying for our expertise *and* for the feeling. So, give it to them. Be a professional ray of sunshine and look out for their emotional experience while they're in your care. It means all nine elements of in-person branding must be in place. For salon people, that means watching that clients don't trip on the styling chair foot rest; it means you need to be especially professional and inviting in your appearance, because clients are so physically close to you. It requires an awareness of the vulnerable position clients put themselves in during their service.

To transfer the concept to a totally different model, let's say yours is a plumbing supply business. Customers aren't asking for help with appearance. Instead, the value you can offer is efficiency. Plumbing contractors care about their time, because every minute spent waiting in your shop is a minute they aren't working to complete their job. If that shop were mine, I would streamline the schedule and inventory to make ordering and picking up as easy and quick as possible.

Think about every interaction customers have in your shop and consider how you can elevate the experience for them. Avoid absolutely any potential pitfall that could associate a negative memory with you. Elevate your service so people walk away raving about you.

RELATIONSHIP BRANDING

No matter who you have in your life, you have a particular brand for every different relationship. For instance, your relationship with your parents is very different from the one you have with your spouse or partner. Business owners have a particular relationship with their team. Confusing that role can cause problems. For example, when a boss goes out with the team on a Friday night for drinks, how are they supposed to step back into the boss role on Saturday morning? If the boss was matching employees, shot for shot, how can they possibly hold an employee accountable for poor performance the next day? When I lost my first team, part of the problem was my familiarity with them. By drinking together and partying with them, I lost a lot of authority over them. Familiarity breeds contempt.

I've talked about Paula before. I've learned so much from her. For years, I played in a local blues-rock band, and Paula would never come to any of my gigs. Others would come watch me play, and I asked her why she didn't want to. She explained, "I don't want to know Band Bennie; I like Work Bennie." I thought she was so wise. Fifteen years on, we're still doing business together, and I've made her a partner.

The segmenting rule goes beyond boss and employee exchanges. Service providers have a particular relationship with their customers too. Think about a therapist. You shouldn't know anything about their personal life, because you are not their friend. They are there to provide a service. In my opinion, it should be the same with hairdressers. Customers shouldn't have to spend their luxury time hearing about their stylist's problems—or anything personal, for that matter. I extend this rule to all business contacts, whether it be business-to-consumer or business-to-business. Keep the relationship professional.

Now, that doesn't mean you can't form bonds or get to know people. It means you should keep your primary purpose in mind. What is the focus of this interaction? What should you both be getting out of it? If I'm too casual in how I approach my business, it will seem unimportant to my customers, and thus the customer will not value it as much.

Paula has a rule about customer relationships too. She recommends that all service providers take control of the conversation as it unfolds. Dental hygienists, veterinarians, landscape maintenance, and hairdressers all see their clients on a regular basis. If the conversation when they see that person veers off into the personal, the provider misses a chance to find another business lead or build the value of the experience in the customer's eyes.

For example, a client sits down and starts talking about what they've been up to. They ask, "Have you seen that new movie?"

"No, I haven't. Have you seen that movie?"

"Yeah, me and my girlfriend went to it the other night."

"Oh really? Who's your girlfriend?"

"Her name's Suzy."

"Have I met Suzy?"

"No, I don't think so."

"Well, what's Suzy's hair like?"

"Oh, it's super curly. She hates it."

"Oh my God! I love doing curly hair! That's one of my favorite types to work on. I would love to do Suzy's hair. Will you tell her to come to me? I would really take good care of her. And please tell her I'm really good."

Do you see how a conversation that could have gone down the road of Hollywood stars instead veered back to the stylist's business? The next time that client sees Suzy, she's going to mention your skill with curly hair. And the client learns that her stylist is a badass with a whole bunch of skills she didn't know about. Because the stylist is intentional in her branding behaviors, she can grow her business.

Keep the priority of building your business in the top of your mind. You already have friends; as a business provider, what you need is more clients. So, control your interactions with clients so your intentions are crystal clear. Be like Paula; keep your personal life separate from your work life.

MOTIVATION
INVERTED PYRAMID

One way to think about your brand is your impact on the world. It's not only how your audience sees you, it's the impact you have on them—how you can have an impact on them. As you grow, your reach grows.

The way I think of my impact in the world is moving upwards on an inverted pyramid. I started impacting one person at a time, cutting hair and talking one-on-one with a customer. Then, I became an employer and helped my staff to learn and earn and support their families. Third on the pyramid for me was manufacturing and distributing. This is a business-to-business level of impact where your reach starts getting to thousands of individuals. As a distributor, I was helping other salon owners grow their businesses…

This is why it's so important to be intentional, because the potential to share, inspire, and teach is massive once it starts growing. Make certain the message you telegraph is the one you intend.

1. Everyone's influence starts out one person at a time.
2. The bigger your business is, the more people you can influence.
3. What message do you want your customers to receive?

AUTHOR & SPEAKER

Infinite potential customers

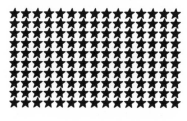

DISTRIBUTOR

Tens of thousands of customers

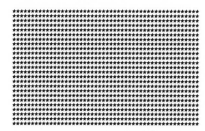

TRAINER & ENTREPRENEUR

100-1000 stylist at a time

SALON OWNER

6 stylists = 6 customer at a time

STYLIST

YOU = 1 customer at a time

THIS IS HOW WE DO IT

I mentioned in Chapter 7 that I script most of the customer interactions my staff uses. They are required to say it the same way every time.

Our phone script is, "Thank you for calling Nova Salon, where we love every hair on your head. This is Bennie. How may I assist you?"

Some people have said that's hokey. I say, the fact they noticed it means they remembered us. We're in their head, and that's a good thing.

Our salon tour is similarly regimented. "This is our design center. We will design a look for you based on your personal image profile. This is the cleansing center; it's where you get to relax while we shampoo your hair and provide a scalp massage. It is our customers' favorite part. This is our color center. These are the restrooms." Anticipate the questions new clients will have so they don't feel uncertain or embarrassed. Do it that way with every new client, every time. The goal is to have the new customer feel like we've been friends for twenty-five years in about four minutes. I want them to be completely at ease when they come visit. It works devastatingly well.

Same thing for every single customer-facing action. When training, I explain, "This is how we seat the customer in the chair, so they don't hit their ankle on the foot rest. This is how we turn the water on for the shampoo. This is how we use water around their hairline, so the shampoo experience is always excellent. This is how we do a shampoo and scalp massage ..." I am a stickler about these procedures, because they are a part of my emotional brand. Every action is calibrated to elevate the customer experience.

The same principles apply in other business models. For instance, there's a new barbeque place in Louisville I visited recently. Typically, at a fast-casual restaurant, the script goes something like, "Here's your order number, we'll call you when it's ready."

This new place blew my socks off. When my order was ready, the gentleman at the counter called my name. I went up to get my food, and he asked, "Have you ever been here before?"

"No, I have not."

"Well, let me tell you all about it. We use an exclusive dry rub that we use on all our meats. We don't have any freezers and don't have any microwaves, because they don't exist. It's all fresh cut, freshly prepared. Remember to take your silverware. Thank you for your business."

Bam! I was so impressed. So, while I ate, I sat close enough to the counter that I could hear how this gentleman proceeded. It was that good every single time. I am constantly studying other business's systems and performance. When I finished eating, I walked up to the counter and told him, "Smokin', brother. Good job."

These interactions are very simple to do, yet very few people go through the effort. When businesses do invest the time, they're making sure their guests are completely at ease—that they know what's going on and have a chance to get their questions answered. That extra effort on the part of the barbeque employee guaranteed that I will be back.

If you're thinking there's no way you could get your employees to be so deliberate about customer interactions, I understand. I get that a lot. I'm going to let you in on a secret. It's all in the training, which leads us to the next chapter.

CHAPTER 12

TRAINING IS BRANDING

WHEN I'M ATTRACTING NEW TALENT, I HEAD OUT TO THE BEAUTY SCHOOLS TO SPEAK. THIS APPROACH IS A WIN-WIN FOR BOTH OF US.

Their students get to hear a seasoned professional explain life in the field. I get a chance to pitch the concept of working for my salon. Probably the biggest, "OhmyGod" responses from those crowds come when they hear how long new hires are considered trainees.

We train new folks for a year before they're released to work on the floor as stylists. I'll explain that process fully in this chapter. First, let me tell you how that conversation at the beauty schools goes.

As I explain our onboarding process, a lot of times I'll hear, "Well, I already got my license, I'm not gonna go take another year to train. Why should I spend all that time sweeping hair and folding towels? I'm ready to start making money now."

So, I ask the room, "How much did y'all pay to go to school here?" It's usually around $18,000.

"So, $18,000 to go to this school to learn how to comb some hair and pass the test and get a license, is that right?"

"Yeah, pretty much."

I'm like, "Well, that's a lot of freakin' money."

"Yeah, that's a lot of money, Bennie."

"So, let me ask you a question. How many of you have ever heard of Vidal Sassoon?" Of course, all the hands go up.

"Of course, we've all head of Vidal Sassoon; he's, like, the god of hairdressing."

"Okay. What would it be worth to study for a year underneath the great Vidal Sassoon?"

"Well, good grief you can't put a price on that. That's ridiculous."

"I totally agree with you. You can't put a value on that, hell, I'll do that today." I do a few more famous names, Paul Mitchell and the Aveda founder, Horst Rechelbacher. Then I explain what I'm getting at.

"You can't put a value on studying a year under those guys; you already spent $18,000 to get your license. Listen to this: I'm going to teach you how to make up to $100,000 a year. Shouldn't you be paying me?"

That approach is strategically brilliant. By that I mean, it weeds out the folks who won't put in the work, and it draws the exact future employee that I'm looking for. Every speech like that I give nets me six or seven top-tier applications.

* * *

Once you have those motivated, earnest young folks, training them correctly is crucial. Actually, training is an arm of your branding process. You can have the most delicious materials in the world, sexy interior design, and a slick website…if your employees don't deliver on the promise of those elements, your brand is a fail. The people representing you are your most important asset. It makes sense to invest time in their training.

At my business, we take our time stepping through the training process, which is broken down into five chunks. As I've already mentioned, I only hire fresh graduates. I want young people, unmarked by other business systems. This way of doing things extends to other business sectors too. Beauty school grads, college grads, or welding school grads—it's all the same. I have found the uninitiated employee integrates better and faster than people who have worked in other salons before.

It's important to note my training protocol only works with a business that has been systemized. It is equally important to instill your systems first in order to facilitate this heightened level of training.

EXPECTATIONS

Expectations must be **extremely clear** to the new hire. Being specific about every single detail sets up the new hire for success. Ambiguity will destroy the new employee. Think about a situation you've been in where you didn't understand what was happening. It's confusing, and you made mistakes. You wore the wrong clothes, asked the wrong questions, and annoyed people, because you just didn't know where you were going. Being out there on your own, without proper training, is like being a tourist in a strange land. If expectations aren't clear, the new person is going to get lost.

I have found the best way to ensure everyone is on the same page is to outline every single requirement in writing. Never assume they know what you want. The first day, we go through the employment contract that includes items like this:

* Expectations of dress code
* Arrive fifteen minutes before your shift
* Safety equipment includes ...
* Proper footwear

We walk through the points, I explain why they are important, then the employee checks the box that acknowledges agreement.

The tone for this training is warm, welcoming, and serious. It's encouraging and no nonsense. It's almost a military-training approach, accomplished in encouraging and straightforward small-group or individual sessions. We're setting the correct energy right up front. It's only fair to do it this way, because you've gotta love 'em enough to make sure there's no ambiguity in communication.

Probably the most important facet of all that conversation is the explanations behind the rules. I train *why* then *how*, for every single thing. Telling them why helps give context to our structure. My critics out there have called my employees Bennibots, as in, "Oh, you don't want to go be a Bennibot. There's no freedom over there." Yes, we require structure; however, I'm not training robots to do what I say. I'm teaching future rock star stylists how to build a quality business.

At the end of the agreement review, both of us sign and date the document so we're on the same page. Is that overly formal? Maybe. I do it this way to signify commitment. You can't pass a check unless you sign it. You can't buy a car without a signature. Any contract you agree to has a spot for your signature at the bottom. In this society, it's understood that your signature means your word.

TRAINING THE BASICS

When I started training staff, I thought about breaking everything good stylists need to know down into bite-sized chunks. We start with what new hires need to know first, which boils down to lessons on our salon culture. After that, there are four other units of training to pass out of: hair color work, highlights, ergonomics, and our signature looks. It takes most people about a year to work through these units. As they work on their training, they're also hustling as apprentices on the floor: sweeping up, doing laundry, and stocking supplies. Some people take longer and some fly through certain skills, so promotion is based on passing skill tests rather than a set amount of time. Some education programs dictate that you must do 200 of these or 400 of those. That's crap. It's a waste of time for a natural. People learn at different speeds: some are faster, and some are slower. Both are fine. Structure needs to be balanced against individuality. To be too regimented about every single thing risks running off talented stylists.

The level of detail each trainee gets for each task they'll need to know is huge. Why do I take so long to promote trainees to client work? Because we're not just cutting hairs here. Stylists who work for me have the potential to earn six-figure salaries. That kind of money improves lives, often drastically. The catch is, to be good at this level—to compete at my level—every single action must be impeccable. My salon attracts the best, most discerning clientele in the region. Learning to meet their expectations takes time. That's okay. Becoming the very best in the industry *should* take time.

After that initial new-employee meeting, we begin the first unit of training: **How to Be an Employee Here**. We talk about what a Nova team member looks like and acts like, and why we do things the way we do. We talk over the goals and mission for the company. Probably most important are the nine elements of in-person branding: eye contact, smile, handshake, wardrobe, scent, posture, dialogue and delivery, punctuality, and attitude. (See Chapter 11 for more.)

We get deep into the details of tasks. For example, most folks would say, "Go sweep over there." We teach new hires how to hold the broom and dust pan for maximum efficiency and discretion. As we do, we talk about the importance of keeping a clean shop. "You see all this hair on the floor? Those are actual body parts down there. For hygiene and for the comfort of guests, we sweep after every client. Hold the dustpan like this so it doesn't fall over and make a racket..."

I know this seems ridiculously simple. Here's the thing though, you cannot assume people know what you know. Go by the rule; if it seems like common sense, it's absolutely necessary to teach it. If you get them on the right track at the beginning, it's so much better than having to fix ingrained errors later. And this approach gives you a chance to observe the new person. As my mom used to say, "If you half-ass this easy job, I can't trust you with anything else, 'cuz you'll half-ass that too." If someone shows pride in sweeping the floor, they'll give the same level of quality to styling customers' hair.

To transfer this onboarding approach to a different industry, think of a plumber's assistant. The first day on the job isn't, "Here's how to fix the ugliest leak you'll ever see." It's "Make certain to put booties on your shoes so you show respect for the customers' homes." In the first days, we're making sure the new hire will be an excellent representative of our brand.

Another element of our training is having the new person teach the learned skill back to the trainer. "I just showed you how to execute our signature shampoo experience, now you teach it back to me." It's much like the method used by doctors teaching hospitals: watch one, do one, and teach one. The ability to teach someone demonstrates deep understanding. Plus, it has made our salon culture flourish, because everyone is required to be a part of the teaching process, as well as apprentices and apprentice managers working together. New employees work with all the staff on their learning. With shampoos, trainees ask staff members if they can practice on them. They keep practicing until a senior staff member has given their approval. Only then can they shampoo paying clients. I feel like this type of exchange is one reason our overall salon culture has flourished. Everybody helps each other. The goal of being lifelong learners becomes self-fulfilling, because we have built our cultural ecosystem around sharing knowledge.

WHY THEN HOW

Just like during the employee agreement meeting, all our teaching gives a why behind our process, as well as a how you do it. For example, as we teach new hires how to do color retouching (the roots on a hair color job) on mannequins, we share the lessons of the best way to do a task. "Hold the color brush like this, so you get the color in the right spot, and you can go faster." We require trainees to show both correct technique and speed before passing out of a new skill. The time element is important, because the whole salon schedule is built around standardized times for each job. If you can't do it fast enough, you're going to have to keep training until you can, because our guests expect timeliness. And our profit structure depends on so many services per day. We're up-front about that so new people understand we're teaching them how to build a profitable business.

🗲
MOTIVATION
PRACTICE WHAT YOU PREACH

While you're setting up a culture of learning and requiring employees to evolve, remember to keep growing yourself. Often times, when we think we know what we're doing, we stop learning and growing. Think about the buds on a plant; new leaves are bright and shiny. They burst with the energy of becoming. That's how new skills feel in your body—exciting and fun. Plus, they make your overall skillset look and feel fresher.

Encourage your staff to show you new things. Go to industry trainings and meetings and learn from your peers. Read voraciously in and out of your industry, because (like this book) small business lessons transfer whether you're styling hair, caring for patients, or laying pipe.

1. Always be learning.
2. Give yourself permission to be a student, even in front of employees.
3. Everyone can be your teacher.

APPRENTICESHIPS

There's a long history of training employees in this methodical fashion. It's only in the modern era of disposable employees that our culture has seen trainings speed up or disappear. In my view, these new hires are going to be in this field their entire lives. There's a lot to know, and our standards are high. We are in good company. When Disney trains employees for a twelve-week summer job, they require substantial training. They do that because their systems are intense and formulated to create a magical experience.

There are many others who *should* train people our way, especially in the professional world. Law grads, med school grads, and dental school grads all have the foundational knowledge of their field. However, they usually didn't study business. They still don't know how to care for clients' or patients' entire experience or how to create a culture that will attract more. Spending your first months of employment under the wing of an expert gives you that expertise.

There's another reason I built an apprentice model. I have designed the salon profit structure, so there is a division between design and labor. It's the same way clothing designers work. Do you think Oscar de la Renta stitched together the mockups he designed? Probably not. He sketched it out, explained it, and assigned the work to an apprentice. The designer designs; the new employee does the labor.

Senior stylists at our level produce $120 to $140 per hour. They cannot attain that level of earning by taking extra time to apply color or perform shampoos. Nor should they be doing the labor; that's the apprentice's job. In this way, the stylist can see more people during their shift, and the upstart gets to spend their training year working up to a higher level under supervision, without the consequences of failure. Without the oversight, the new hairdresser would flame out and possibly leave the profession. With the correct training and systems, the income opportunity is tremendous. That's what I'm offering—and my stylists who have been with me for years like it that way.

GRADUATION

From experience, I have learned to let my graduated trainees work slowly to a full stylist schedule. I used to clear folks out of apprenticeship and give them forty hours a week to cut and style hair. They were excited at first, but it didn't take long to find those new folks complaining in the back room. They went from hourly trainee pay (plus tips) to a wide-open schedule of nothing. They're new enough not to have any established clients yet. Everyone they've worked on up until now has been someone else's client.

Let me tell you, idle hands truly are the devil's workshop. I've heard more bitching and complaining from people in that position than any other phase of employment. Unfortunately, if I leave them there, fuming about how they're not getting any business, they'll disappear into a black hole of entitlement and never come out again.

These days, I give new stylists one day per week to take clients and keep them in the assistant role their other days. That way, they're getting a chance to fly free and it keeps them completely engaged, without giving up all the time and tips from shampooing and applying color. "You show me you can get customers in that chair on your one day. Once that day is full, I'll tell the front desk to open a second day and funnel you some clients." I'm communicating that they need to earn the privilege of a full schedule. It's their role to bring in new business, not mine. Once that starts happening, *then* I share the wealth.

NUTS & BOLTS
BE POSITIVE

The culture we live in can be fairly negative. That's unfortunate because when we exert energy talking about the things that are wrong or should be different, we're actually reinforcing the negative concept. Why not just state the positive idea instead? When talking to a little kid most people say, "Don't drop that milk." That just makes him think more about the milk falling to the floor. Instead say, "Hold tight with two hands." Then his hands *and* his brain are working together to keep the cup where it ought to be.

The concept effects us adults as well. For example, I could train a new person this way: "Don't bend over to reach the client's hair." Or, I could say, "Use the chair hydraulics to bring the client up to you." Do you see how the first statement cements an image of hunching in my trainee's imagination and the other reinforces the correct ergonomics?

I believe the word don't can be overused. It's a missed opportunity to tell a positive story. So often, arguments give you a "not this, but that" approach. Or, "Don't do this, do that." If I'm trying to go forward, I can't be looking backward in the rear-view mirror. Use the positive idea and stop.

1. Don't say don't. ☺
2. Use positive statements instead.
3. Take the opportunity to tell beneficial stories.

CHAPTER 13

ASK AND YE SHALL RECEIVE: MARKETING

IF YOU THINK OF BUILDING YOUR BUSINESS KIND OF LIKE BUILDING A HOUSE—BRANDING, TRAINING, AND MARKETING ARE THE FOUNDATION, WALLS, AND ROOF.

You can brand and bring customers in, but if your staff isn't trained to make a serious impression, your branding was a fail. Like a roof, a marketing plan is necessary. However, as I learned when *Glamour* called, you can market yourself right out of business. Back then, our standards and practices weren't solid, and when the crowds appeared, we were not ready. You really do need all three elements to be rock solid in order to have a stellar finished product.

When most folks say marketing, they're talking about advertising. I operate differently. Outside of running ads when I rebranded the business from Hair by Bennie and Friends to Nova Salon, I have hardly ever paid for an ad. Why? Because, I have learned that personal connections are far superior. Almost all of our new clients at the salon come from our existing client base. That's not by chance; we planned it that way, because those folks are trained to expect a superior product—and they're willing to pay for it. They're the exact type of client I want. It stands to reason that their friends and family are going to have a similar set of values. However—and this is key—you can't just hope those loyal clients will do your work for you.

The number one idea that most business people completely ignore is this: **ask for business.** You have to ask before you receive. All good marketing campaigns include an ask of some sort.

"Call your State Farm Agent today."

"Have a Coke and a smile."

"Got milk?"

We're all pretty used to these tags at the end of ads; however, the small-business owner has an advantage over national brands—we know our clients well and can ask for business referrals face-to-face.

Here's what most people get wrong; that request for business must be direct. It won't work if you say to a client on their way out the door, "Hey, I'd love to see your friends here too." It's got to be clear, well practiced, and direct. "Hey, Sally, [pause] I *really* like doing your hair. Will you please send me your friends and family?" Remember, leave space in that sentence so their ears will listen harder to hear what's coming next. Use different inflection to stress the important words. Think of your personal communications as a musical phrase, with rests and varied notes.

FOCUS YOUR TARGET

While you're asking, think hard about *who* you should be asking. If marketing is the pursuit of new business, it's important to zero in exactly on what type of new business you want. Here's how I see the hierarchy of potential new clients.

Walk In: That's the least valuable client to me. My philosophy is this: if they're going to walk into my business, they'll walk into someone else's business the next time. You can't leave that to chance. To me, a walk-in isn't the best customer. I want to attract clients who value my work, who will pay what it's worth, and will come back again and again.

Salon Referral: This might be a client who heard about me in a news story or saw my website. Those folks aren't excited enough about what I offer for me to spend a lot of time aiming for them. That's a big reason why I don't run ads as a general rule. It's hard to translate the experience I offer to print or radio.

Client Referral: Sally's friends are coming in, because she's told them how fantastic we are. Those client referrals are valuable, certainly. Many businesses think of those new customers as their holy grail; however, I say we can do even better than that.

The number one strategy that has helped build Nova Salon to what it is today is a process we call the **Styling Lab™**. This method has greater retention than any of these other four. I want clients who want my expertise and an exceptional experience. Not only do I go looking for them, I create them. When all is said and done, I want them to see me as the go-to expert. That is my goal.

FREE KNOWLEDGE: THE BEST WAY TO WIN CLIENTS

The best marketing technique I ever discovered is a thing I've been doing since the mid-80s: free education events. In Chapter 4, I mentioned the classes I taught at the modeling agency and school. Teaching girls how to properly shampoo and comb out their hair led to their mothers being loyal clients. Education can lead to gargantuan growth.

It's so effective that I have continued to use that approach throughout my career. In the same era as those girls' classes, I approached the local tennis club (kind of like a country club) and offered a class for their members. The membership manager loved the idea; she needed events and benefits to offer, so she put me in the newsletter. The day of the event, I arrived to find a room filled with 100 affluent women, waiting to hear me talk. Wow! That was more than I expected. I ducked into a bathroom, puked, then took a deep breath. I used all the charm and speaking abilities I knew and taught those ladies to comb out tangles. The next day, my salon phone went nuts.

That was a huge win, so I thought I'd try it again at an expensive apartment complex in town. The manager okay'd the idea, set a date, and put a flyer in mailboxes. The day of, I brought in a veggie tray and started prepping the space. Management said they expected about twenty-five people. Nice, I thought. The door opened...and eight to ten gray-haired ladies, all pushing walkers, shuffled in. Oohh. I hadn't done my due diligence and researched the population. Too late, I realized that the plan I had for teaching about scrunching and blow-drying curly hair wasn't going to cut it. So, I regrouped. I said to myself, "I'm going to make this one of the most wonderful afternoons these ladies ever saw." And I did. We had a great time. I didn't get a single customer from the group; however, they loved it. And so did I.

I include this failed event as an example to illustrate the point that not everything you do will be a home run. That's okay. Everyone is important. Whether you get two or eighty people at your program, they deserve to be treated beautifully. Always do your best.

The education events have evolved over the years; however, the core is still the same. To expand a stylist's business, the stylist chooses a favored client (the type of person they want more of) to host an event at our salon for their friends and family. Essentially, it's a hair party we host in the salon, after hours. We offer education and gifts at an exclusive event, designed just for them. This is the Styling Lab™.

This concept grew out of an idea I borrowed from the book *The Man Who Sold America* by Jeffrey L. Cruikshank and Arthur W. Schultz. The book details the career of Albert D. Lasker, one of the first ad men in the twentieth century. One of the lessons I most identified with in this biography was the concept of education as advertising. Lasker designed a campaign for a beer company that was based around the concept of showing how it was done. The ads talked about the beer company's special way of combining pure water, wheat, and hops. They romanced that dialog a bit, created some magic around the process, and it was hugely successful. All of a sudden, this beer company was a big deal in the market. Here's what I love about that approach; they were making beer exactly the same way as everyone else. It was their willingness to pull the curtain back that won consumer loyalty. It was like they said, "We'll show you how we do it, and we'll show you how much we care about quality." It was their transparency and goodwill that won people over.

That spirit of generosity and desire to earn trust is exactly what we convey in a Styling Lab™. Though the intent is the same as Lasker's campaign, I believe we have even better ROI, because the connection all happens face to face. The first step to a Styling Lab™ is for a stylist to talk with an established client about inviting eight or so friends to the event.

"Mary, you're a great client. I'd like to invite you to one of our styling labs as a way of saying thank you."

The next question is always, "What's a styling lab?"

We have found that the way we describe the experience is crucial. Because women have all been to something like a houseware party; they know that there's a cloud of obligation over the night. Most times, guests have to buy something so the host (who spent all day cleaning like crazy) earns enough points to receive the hostess gift. So, we're sure to explain exactly what our intent is, up front.

"A Styling Lab is an informal gathering where we have all your girlfriends and co-workers—I know you sing in a group—I'd love to have all them as customers too. We'll have an evening of demonstration, sharing professional techniques and tips with you. It gives me a chance to meet new customers. And it's a wonderful ladies' night out."

Then the customer asks, "How much?"

"It's absolutely complementary. It's my way of saying thank you for being a great customer, and my way of introducing myself to all your friends and get new customers."

It's important to let the client know you're doing it for a reason. One, I really appreciate you as a customer. And two, I want to grow my business with people who are like you. We don't want clients to walk away with lingering doubts about a hidden agenda. We tell them right up front why we're making the invitation. Once she says yes, and many people do, it's just logistics after that.

We do not want the customer to work. The stylist makes it as easy as possible for the client, either taking charge of the invites through an email list or letting the client do so if she prefers. We set the night, the time, and we like to set a count. (Never just open up a night and say, "Y'all come." Make someone accountable for the guest list.) We have found that events like this work best on Monday through Thursday evenings, somewhere between 6:30 and 8:00 p.m.

The night of the event, plan twenty minutes for arriving, snacking (provide wine and cheese or the equivalent), and networking. Then, take charge of the floor. Once everyone is seated introduce yourself, then make everyone feel like they're included through a story. Always begin with a story. One common anecdote I use is something that happened to a client of the salon.

"A young lady comes into the salon one day. She's got a hoodie on, though it wasn't even that cold outside. She takes the hoodie off and she has a round brush stuck so tight all the way to her head—I mean it was in there. We couldn't get it out. We wound up having to cut it out, right?" That's the start of my program.

Then I ask, "How many of you have ever had a round brush stuck?" Almost all their hands go up.

I start with a story like that because the mind listens for the familiar. Once we hear something we can relate to, we're automatically more comfortable. Then, I give my talk about proper hair care. I literally act out how to shampoo hair as I narrate the process. "You get up in the morning; you know about six o'clock; you got all the stuff to do; and you go into the shower; and you get in there and turn the water on; you do the glamourous shower moves like you see on TV and ..." I paint an entire picture for them, and they see the whole thing. Then I get down to the nuts and bolts and teach them how to actually work with the shampoo, how to condition properly, and the next steps.

Most importantly, I'll pull someone from the audience. Maybe there's someone in the group whose hair is looking fuzzy. I know that two minutes with a dryer and round brush will dramatically change her look. I'll say, "Hey, Tracy, would you come up here for a second."

Tracy's friends all cheer her on, and when she's finished, the adoration from her peers is enormous. Tracy feels great, her friends are happy for her, and I just jumped to hair god status in their eyes. That's when I'll go further on selling services. I'll say, "Now y'all—do you think Tracy would look good with a few subtle highlights around her face; it would make her eyes really shine, don't you think?" The audience, of course, says, "YES!" Suddenly, Tracy is ready to book an appointment for highlights—and so are a couple of her friends.

Let me be clear about sincerity. I only recommend changes that would look good. The salesmanship I employ during these demos is aimed at showing my skill as a stylist to attract new customers who want it. I'm not trying to sell something people don't want (or get a whole bunch of people in the door who are only there for a discount). To be able to transfer excitement that increases sales is an art form. These demos are a chance for me to show my skills, to build trust, and to teach a technique the audience can use. When we're finished with the demos, I have illustrated that I do know what I'm talking about, that I'm willing to share my knowledge, and—when they need a new hair person—I'm a good bet.

This experience is what makes Styling Lab™ clients my holy grail clients. Clients we win through these events have greater retention than walk-ins and salon referrals—even more than client referrals. As I said before, I want top-shelf clients. I won't get those people in my door through advertising or running promotions. The kind of client that comes in for 20% off is not the client I want. I want the one who respects me as a professional. Allowing people the chance to witness my ability, at no cost, builds their confidence and their willingness to trust me with their appearance.

As we're getting ready to close, we do a call to action, which is carefully rehearsed before the event. A winning pitch includes a certain body movement, an opening up of the shoulders, an extension of one hand, a smile, and a warm tone of voice. If you're not sure what that looks like, Google a body language video. Watch him or her move the audience to action. That level of polish doesn't happen accidentally. We rehearse it, and we train it into our bodies, so it feels natural on stage.

For the Styling Labs™ that call to action is a 50% [pause] one-time-only discount on services booked that night, available to the guests and the host of the evening. In addition, we offer a discount on products purchased that night. It sounds simple, but I'm here to tell you these practices win like crazy. A stylist who takes the extra time has just won six to eight new clients.

We encourage other small businesses to steal this idea, because it's just obscene how well it works. And you don't have to be a hairdresser to use the concept.

NUTS & BOLTS
USE THE NEURAL PATHWAYS

Have you ever bought a car and then noticed there are dozens of them around? You tirelessly researched just the right car—narrowed down to the very best one for you. Then, you start driving it around, and suddenly it's everywhere! This is your perirhinal cortex at work. That's the part of the brain that evolved to search for the familiar. I'm sure this instinct was a huge help to our ancestors for finding food sources they knew to be safe. In modern society, we're still constantly searching for the familiar, whether it's the song we keep hearing—or that face in the crowd we're sure we've seen before.

This sense of the familiar can also be used to help people feel comfortable in your place of business. When I'm doing a seminar, I try to immediately set an audience at ease by sharing a familiar story, so I can have deeper communication with them. I may be talking about power of scent and use the example of a common client, the lady with terrible breath. Everyone knows at least one dragon lady.

When I tell that story, the whole room is there with me, because it's familiar to them. When I tell the story about seeing young girls, one of whom stooped as she walked, everyone nods. They've all seen that person—or have been that person. When communicating, the more we use familiar patterns, the more we connect on a deep level.

That's why our phone script at Nova Salon is, "Thank

you for calling Nova Salon, where we love every hair on your head. My name is Bennie. How may I assist you?"

That phrase, every hair on your head, is something almost all Southern mamas say about their kids. They say, "Oh, my boy. I love every hair on his head." Another salon I've trained for years answers the phone this way. "Thank you for choosing Studio 11, where you're more than a ten." Clients who hear that script are immediately more connected and more engaged.

1. Human brains constantly scan for the familiar.
2. Use that instinct to your advantage.
3. Find familiar stories, phrases, songs, and scents to help you bond immediately with clients.

BEYOND THE SALON

To transfer the free-education concept to another industry, look no further than Home Depot. The clinics they offer in-house are another way to do this sort of grassroots marketing. A small business owner of any kind can do the same thing. Think about the thing your clients ask for over and over; giving them that knowledge is a sign of goodwill. Here's my famous taco recipe; here's how to change out a kitchen faucet; here's how you design your own tattoo; here's how to properly check your dogs for ticks or trim their nails. Nine times out of ten your audience won't do those things themselves. Or they'll be able to do the small technique but will want help taking the next step. And who will they call for that expertise? The person who has already shown their mastery in that area—the person who earned their trust by giving away some knowledge for free.

In a world swimming with free information on YouTube and blogs, you have to make your event more than an informational clinic. What can people get at your place they can't find from the comfort of their couch? The answer is a social event. A fun night with friends, refreshments, and the chance to experience something new together can't be searched up on the internet. This works especially well with a group of women, because they're more open to cheering for and encouraging each other. However, the concept transfers to a male-dominated demographic as well. The master craftsman opening up his secrets is a powerful draw. This is a chance to see behind the curtain. Here's how you get a clean line between paint colors; here's how you build the ideal video gaming computer; here's how you shave without causing a rash... Insider knowledge gets a wow factor that builds an appreciation among the audience members.

What you're doing by creating this sort of experience is building credibility and winning loyalty. You want your clients to walk away with a sense of ownership. When they talk to acquaintances, they're bursting to share their connection.

"Call my guy."

"You should go see my gal."

"My" is the operative word there. When they use it about your business, it means they have taken a vested interest in your success. It also means your phone is about to ring.

HERE'S THE CHALLENGE

Of those reading this book, only one percent will attempt to build education events into their marketing plan. The reason why is because so many people are scared to death of public speaking. Have courage. It's a skill that can be learned.

Your events are going to be geared around providing a service. Let me explain. This goes back to understanding why you're up there on the stage in the first place. You are helping people. By being of service, you can feel confident in your approach. You can feel good about providing something people will appreciate. As Paula, my rock star says, "How do you build self esteem? Help someone out, every day."

MOTIVATION
SPEAK NOW

Being able to present one's ideas changes the world. I mean that literally. Public speaking sways entire populations of people (for good and bad). It's a powerful skill set to own. If you don't feel comfortable speaking, that's even more of a sign that you need to do it.

Common advice to conquer a fear of public speaking is to picture the audience naked. I don't recommend that; however, at its heart, there is a kernel of truth in that crackpot practice. **Understand that those in your audience are regular people like you.** They're sitting in uncomfortable plastic chairs staring at you, because they want to learn what you know.

Think of a speech as an opportunity to help others. You're the expert; you have a passion about your field or talent. Probably the biggest speaking barrier, even for experienced business people, is a fear of being judged inadequate or stupid. I want to encourage you to be your own cheerleader. You don't know what audience members are thinking, and you shouldn't assume it's negative. As you rehearse, visualize your speech inspiring your audience. See them smiling and clapping for you.

Before you begin the speech, loosen your body up. Stretch your arms, shoulders, and sides, so you can breathe easily. Align your feet, hips, and shoulders with your head so there's a flow of energy from the crown of your head to the soles of your feet. Now breathe deeply into your diaphragm…and go get 'em.

1. Judge yourself worthy of sharing your knowledge.
2. Transfer your energy around your topic of expertise.
3. Breathe.

CHAPTER 14

THINKING ABOUT THINKING

I'VE BEEN THINKING ABOUT WRITING THIS BOOK FOR NEARLY TWO DECADES.

I wanted to share some of my early stories, because I know from my speaking experiences they can inspire other people. I wanted to demonstrate that difficult circumstances do not limit your potential—that success is not determined by your environment. The idea here is: I made it; therefore, you can too.

When the inspiration first occurred, I had to get my mom's permission to tell the story, since it's part hers. That took a while. Sadly, she passed away shortly after we began, and progress stopped. Time passed, business continued to grow, and the book still lingered in my imagination. When I finally reached a point where I was ready to rock and roll, another barrier popped up. It was completely internal; however, it was probably the hardest hurdle to clear.

On the day I had planned to finally set words on paper, an emotional punch reached up and whacked me. Hundreds of doubts swarmed to the surface of my consciousness. My head flooded with all these questions. "Who the hell do you think you are? Who's going to believe your advice? You're not qualified to write a book …"

It was the remnants of my former self, trying like hell to get me to stop growing. I almost quit, but then I told myself to sit the fuck down and get to work. I took a deep breath and moved forward with the project, one step at a time.

When fear starts having its way with your agenda, it's important to recognize what's going on. An acronym for FEAR might be: false evidence appearing real. Sometimes false statements your mind throws up do seem real. Though we like to consider our adult selves as evolved and mature, underneath the polish, we're all just big bushel baskets of our influences and experiences. We're conditioned to doubt—to frequently stop and wonder if our decisions are correct.

I trace those voices directly to early childhood. In the Chapter 9 motivation box, "Don't Believe Everything You Think", I covered the echoes of our parents' voices that constantly shouted, "No, stop, don't!" Those childhood warnings are valid ways to keep young kids out of the street. If you watch a two or three-year-old child, they tear through the world like they're not afraid of anything. By about age six, kids slow down some. They've been indoctrinated in fear. By that point, how many times has that kid been told, "No, stop, don't! Get over here." The words come from a place of love, yet those cautions persist long after we've grown. How many times is that same child told, "Go for it! You can do it. Rock it; go get it." For most of us, the answer is: not often enough.

Those warnings continue unchecked in many adults. I ran across a great example of this conditioning recently. A woman in a consulting session was scared to death to open her own salon. Even though she was qualified, she was absolutely terrified to take that step. Like this woman, in order to grow, we have to recognize that there are internal influences fighting against our desires. Noticing that doubt is the first step.

We must recognize where all that stimuli and input came from. Who exactly wants us to "be careful, don't get hurt"? That's where the three questions (discussed in Chapter 8) come in.

1. Where did that thought come from?
2. Is it true?
3. Will it help me, or hurt me?

Those are the first two tools you can use to build awareness of your inner dialog and start to change it. To see past your prevailing attitudes, you have to be aware of how your mind works. Those attitudes are why you are where you are. At the end of the day: **we never get what we want; we get what we are.**

So often, what we are is the same thing our parents were—and their parents before them. Because you are reading this now, you have the chance to halt a negative pattern that originated from your family, teachers, peers, or even the media. The cautions that were repeated by your parents are the same ones that were ingrained in them as children. Your grandparents were probably told the same things. As grown kids, we're simply carrying the same bucket of water around that our parents carried, and their parents carried, and so on. As they mature, kids start holding worries that belong to other people. The beliefs are not theirs, yet their life plays out according to them—usually unconsciously.

Here's another example from my life. In my family, my mother and all her siblings were brought up to believe in the value of hard work. Sounds admirable, right? The flipside of that is not one person emphasized the importance of education. Education wasn't a word I ever heard from my mom, my aunts, or my grandma. They told all of us cousins to get a job. "You've gotta get a job. Make yourself some good money; you've got to make money." Out of nine aunts and uncles and all their children, there are three college graduates in our family. That culture is a big reason I went to beauty school; it was fast, and I saw that I could earn right away. I don't regret that decision, but I'm citing the example here to show how the list of options for kids gets pared down by who raises them.

Unlearning all that parental conditioning *is* possible. Parents themselves can help with a bit of that, or a teacher, older sibling, or even social media to an extent. Awareness and questioning are the keys. The inner conversation might sound like, "Wait a minute; that's not true at all." That's where the three questions come in, which can lead to this self-discovery. "Because it's true for Mom, doesn't mean it's true for me. Just because it was true for Grandpa, I don't have to carry that."

WRITE YOUR OWN PROGRAM

The way I think of it, our inner dialog is much like a computer program. Let's say I'm keeping books with financial software. I punch in all the numbers then ask for a financial report. When it comes out, it's all wrong. What the hell? Well, it's wrong because I entered the information incorrectly. The software didn't do anything wrong, it just gave me back what I put in. The mind is exactly the same way. Garbage in, garbage out. No more, no less. If your mind is inundated with the mantra: "No! Stop! Don't!" it will repeat that until we consciously change the programming. "I can. I will. I must."

If you get only one thing from this chapter, let it be this: **You can change your inner beliefs.** As little kids, other people write our program. Then, we start taking over, running our program. Often, that program plays out in ways we don't like. We yell more than we would like to. We watch TV rather than develop healthier routines. We're afraid to raise prices on our services.

That's the program running as written. The messages that built those behaviors might sound something like: I yell because I have an Irish temper; I'm binge-watching because nothing ever changes anyway; I can't raise prices, no one's going to pay that much money. Look at your relationships, your physical well-being, and your bank account...all those results you witness **are**

based on your very best thinking. Your thoughts created every one of those outcomes.

Sometimes we don't even know that we don't like the results, because we think this life is reality. People say, "I'm a realist. This is just how things are." A statement like that is a red flag to me. It's a sure sign that a person has accepted a limited vision of their potential. Like my family's attitude about education, jobs and vocational training were the only recognized path. That was "just how life works" for them. I'm fortunate that I had innate talents that worked well in this field, and I'm grateful for my family. My point is, if I had been the type of kid who dreamed of building rocketships or caring for the horses at Churchill Downs, life would have been much harder for me, because engineering and veterinary jobs require college degrees.

Living inside a pre-set bubble can be hard to escape. Hopefully something triggers a thought or behavior, and we notice our pattern. Once that little bit of awareness starts to happen it's a wow moment. It could be a fluke. It could be a teacher somewhere that says, "You're important, kid. I believe in you." Where at home it's, "You're no good. You're no son of mine." That's a chance for the person to think, "Wait a minute…I'll be damned. I've been brainwashed."

MAKE A NEW SCRIPT

Once noticed, the old scripts that run like tapes in our head can be changed. If your old way of being was a script written in childhood, you can also write a new version. In fact, writing down the plan is an excellent way to begin. What are your dreams for yourself? Put it down on paper. Once you have some concrete ideas of what you *do* want versus what you *don't* want, you are ready for my best tool – visualization.

In my dressing area, I have several sheets of paper taped to the wall. On them are my new script. As I get ready each day, I recite those statements aloud. "I am a real estate investor," is an old favorite. This financial affirmation is a great contrast against the way many people often set about making change. Often times, folks who want to get out of debt might say, I'm going to pay this off, then this, then this.

I absolutely support getting out of debt. However, debt used correctly has launched many businesses. My only quibble is in the phrasing of the goal. When we say it the second way, the mind hears, "I'm going to" rather than "I am ..." Remember, the unconscious mind is a computer program that merely follows instructions. "I'm going to" really means not yet. It keeps that person in a constant state of paying off. Sometimes people even incur more debt to maintain the program—and they don't even know why they're working against their own interests! That's why we need to make "I am" statements.

"I am a homeowner."

"I am debt free."

"I own a forty million dollar per year company."

"I create wealth."

Write them as if they have already occurred.

Say your statement aloud each day so your unconscious mind can hear. Put your hand on your heart so your sense of touch gets involved and ingrains the message. **Say your goal as if it has already happened.** Say it every day.

This is how to create intentional change and re-program your mind. It works because, as you venture out into your day, your mind is in a doing mode. You start to notice opportunities you wouldn't have before. There's a new willingness to take risks because your mind already thinks of itself as doing those new things. For example, when trying to lose weight, you might say, "I exercise every day." Then, when it's time to hit the gym, your brain thinks, "Yup. Hitting my goal again." Whereas, if the statement is,

"I will exercise." That could be tomorrow—or next year sometime. There's no discomfort in skipping a workout, because the goal is set for someday, as opposed to right now.

While we're talking about internal dialog, pay attention to the way you speak to yourself. Negative self-talk is just as effective as positive. For example, people who lose their keys may say, "Darn it! I always lose my keys." The unconscious will hear that, and it takes the statement literally. If you say things like that to yourself, you'll forget your keys every damn time. Or they lock their keys in the car and realize it just as the door clicks shut. "I'm such an idiot!" they might say. Other unkind things people often repeat to themselves are: I'm so fat; I look old; I suck, I'm such a loser, etc.

Would you walk up to a stranger on the street and say any of those things? Of course not! It's rude. So why say them to yourself? You are the most important person you can speak to—make sure the words are kind. Insults are heavy to carry around, and they have a way of writing a surreptitious script that you don't want to play out. If you don't actively root those out, **you won't be living your story, your story will be living you.**

Now, just because reciting affirmations seems like a simple thing to do, does not mean that these efforts will be easy. This is not Pollyanna, nor is it for the meek. Your old programs will fight for control, just like mine did when I started writing this book. "You might even think to yourself, this is dumb. This won't work." Again, that's your old self trying to hold you back. I get it, it's uncomfortable to imagine yourself another way. It's scary for your less-evolved self to let go of old ways. Doubts will start yammering away in your head, asserting the old narrative. Ignore those voices. Your fear doesn't get to steer the ship; you do. Be patient and have faith. It takes time to undo years of negative programming. Remember that your mind can go there if you allow it to. When you understand and trust yourself, it will be done.

I have been using this visualization technique since I learned about it from Zig Ziglar in the 80s. All of my old goals from the dressing room wall have come to pass. I grew my businesses. I learned to speak in front of big crowds. I started new revenue streams. I started a band. I wrote this book. All of those things happened through visualization first. And, I'll tell you, it was—and is—a lot of emotional work. Wrestling doubts is heavy lifting. The hardest part of building my business was not finding investors or scrimping pennies. It was having personal faith…and sticking to the vision long enough to get through the dip.

What's the dip? Most people quit right before they get what they want. Think about it: a new business launches with a lot of hoopla and excitement. When the emotional high wanes, reality sets in and things get hard. It's like they're in the wilderness; they're wrestling alligators: the hard stuff rises up. That's when most people quit. If they can just persevere beyond the low point and up to the other side of the valley, the big picture becomes clear. In business, that could be—and usually is—several years. If it's taking you a long time, that's okay. The fact that you're reading this book means that you're seeking and learning. That effort means you're coming up on the other side of the valley.

KEEP REACHING

You'll notice that I've been writing and saying my goals out loud for many years, and I haven't stopped. It's not that it took me thirty years to build a profitable business; it didn't. I keep following this practice, because every goal achieved is a chance for me to reach higher. The first script was small; then my mind expanded, and I learned to see a bit broader in scope. That next script was small compared to where I am now. Five years ago, I was aiming for two million dollars per year in revenue; now I'm thinking about $100 million. I hope that in ten years my current set of daily affirmations will seem tiny compared to where I have grown. Like stepping stones, the scripts expanded as my experiences and imagination did. The goals got incrementally better as I went along.

I can say definitively that I am a different man today than I was yesterday. One way I know this is I can read a book today that I read even two years ago and it's like a whole new book. I'm going back to stuff I read in the 80s that is monumental for me today. It's one more example of how when the mind starts to mature; then your ability to see more broadly expands.

Now, don't mistake my desire for perpetual growth and learning for constant dissatisfaction. I'm deeply proud of what I have accomplished. I have learned that I am my happiest when I'm aiming for a new goal. You might ask, "Will I ever have enough?" To that I say, it has nothing to do with the money. The money is just the scorecard to track progress. I'm never going to stop, because if I did it would cap my potential. My ultimate goal is continuous personal growth and simultaneously helping others find their own path to growth.

I have also learned that **success is only important until you have it.** Back when I was a young man, I wanted to prove myself. Now that I have done that, it's like, "Okay. Next?" Staying in that mode with a chip on my shoulder would be unhealthy. The reason I continue moving forward is because I've been blessed with talents. I have a responsibility to use those gifts for the betterment of my fellow man.

It didn't start out so virtuously. I set out as a young man on a mission to prove my family wrong about my innate abilities. Then I needed to prove the same to myself. I don't have anything left to prove now. I just want to see who else I can help to dream big and to provide for their families. Hopefully, they'll do the same and pass it on. And on and on the blessings will flow.

MOTIVATION
WHAT ARE YOUR GHOSTS TELLING YOU?

Motivational speaker, Les Brown, gives a speech that I absolutely love. He says, "Imagine being on your death bed. Standing around your bed are the ghosts of the ideas, the dreams, the abilities, the talents given to you by life." Brown goes on to imagine what a tragedy it would be if this imagined person hadn't acted on those gifts...hadn't taken the trip, didn't start the business, was too afraid to write the book. **What a waste that would be.** Those solutions and inspirations will never come to be now, because they died with the person.

No matter your walk of life, it's very important to look within yourself and see what assets you've been given. It is your responsibility to nurture and use them. Help them contribute to the world. Not everyone has the level of talent that you do. You must share them with the world. It is your personal responsibility to do so. No matter your walk of life, look within, and see what assets you have. Then imagine how they can be used for the betterment of all mankind.

1. Recognize what God gave you for the gift it is.
2. Nurture and grow your talents.
3. Leave this world a better place.

FAITH

When Europe emerged from the age of enlightenment, everyday people suddenly saw answers (and tools for seeking answers) replacing their confusion. They could no longer retreat into the muddle, because they couldn't un-know the lessons of philosophy, math, and science. I hope you've had an enlightenment of sorts from reading this book. Now that you've read this book, you can't unlearn the lessons. Now you know about the power of your unconscious, about the importance of lifting others up, and about your responsibility as an employer of others to lead—now that you are aware, it means you are responsible for the knowledge.

Beyond all the lessons about small business, I hope you take away the truth: **you are in charge of your own destiny**. Regardless of your past or where you came from, your future is entirely up to you. I hope you come away from this book with the faith in yourself to take control of your future.

It would have been very easy for me to spend my whole life only known as the kid whose mom killed his dad. In fact, there were many who anticipated exactly that for my life. Carrying that shadow wouldn't have served anyone. Putting down burdens from your past is possible for you too. Whatever your encumbrance—deep, dark, or ugly—it has nothing to do with the rest of your life. Your position today has absolutely nothing to do with where you're going tomorrow, and the past is so far removed from you—it's irrelevant.

The bad news about life is you're responsible.
The good news about life is you're responsible.

You're the boss of you. Now that you're here with me, sit still and think about what tomorrow will look like. See your future as you would like it to be. You've got to see it first, and you must believe you can achieve it in order to move forward.

That's how Olympians do it. I think Michael Phelps won all his medals sometime in the eighth grade. He physically received them in his 20s and 30s, but they were real to Phelps long before that. I'm talking about Olympic thinking. It's the way the diver mentally choreographs every single muscle twitch, including surfacing and seeing the score board covered in 10s. That mental practice is way more important than the physical workouts, because—without it—doubt creeps us and sabotages us. The success story will be yours as well. You'll win profits and awards way before you'll be acknowledged for them. Through mental practice, you win before you win.

Society thinks about a middle-class existence as normal; that's false. There's nothing normal about being in the middle. That has nothing to do with reality. The world needs bigger thinkers. There are already so many small players. The world needs you to become more. Not everyone has to be a Steve Jobs or Warren Buffet, but each individual has an ability or skill set that could move their community forward.

The key to using the talent is: think about other people. "What can I do for you? How can my ideas promote your well-being?"

It's Zig again. "If you want to achieve your goals, help others achieve theirs."

The responsibility is on your shoulders now. Start the project. Build the house. Write the book. Lift the people. Let's go! The act of doing it will change you forever. The work will change you into the person you desire to be.

It has me.

RECOMMENDED READING

How to Win Friends and Influence People by Dale Carnegie

Rich Dad, Poor Dad: What the Rich Teach Their Kids About Money That the Poor and Middle Class Do Not! by Robert Kiyosaki

See You at the Top by Zig Ziglar

Swim with the Sharks Without Being Eaten Alive: Outsell, Outmanage, Outmotivate, and Outnegotiate Your Competition by Harvey McKay

Think and Grow Rich by Napoleon Hill

The 10 X Rule: The Only Difference Between Success and Failure by Grant Cardone

21 Irrefutable Laws of Leadership by John C. Maxwell

ACKNOWLEDGMENTS

A special thanks to all those who have had the courage to start small businesses before me, and to those to come. *Rock & Roll.*

24909010R00131

Made in the USA
Columbia, SC
01 September 2018